Digital Transformation in the First Person

Surviving and thriving in a hypercompetitive era.

Jim Love and Fawn Annan

Copyright © 2019 James Love and Fawn Annan
All Rights Reserved
ISBN-9781688210363

Dedication

To the staff of IT World Canada (ITWC) and Amazing! Agency both current and past who have built and continue to build and transform this iconic Canadian company.

To all of those who work in Canada's ICT industry. Yours is the community we proudly serve.

To both our spouses Jim Annan and Linda Love who have had faith in us over all these years. You've believed in us and continue to inspire us to rise to the challenges that face us.

TABLE OF CONTENTS

FOREWORD — I

THE AGE OF ACCELERATED INNOVATION — 1

OUR STORY — 37

STOP THE PRESSES! — 41

TRANSFORM OR DIE — 53

THE DOT-CUSTOMER — 69

OUTRUN THE BEAR — 87

BUILDING AN AGILE INFRASTRUCTURE — 115

CULTURE — 147

WHAT WE DID — 169

WHAT WE LEARNED — 187

RESOURCES — 203

Foreword

For people who have made their career in the technology industry, IT World Canada is an iconic Canadian business to business (B2B) publisher. In the world of consumer publications and to those outside the industry it may be virtually unknown. But within Canada's technology industry the covers of its Canadian CIO magazine were the tech-sector equivalent of the 'cover of the Rolling Stone.' When your picture hit the cover, you had indeed 'made it' in the Canadian industry. While the Canadian CIO magazine was its flagship, the company spawned myriad niche technology publications such as *Network World Canada*, *Computerworld Canada, Computer Dealer News* (now *Channel Daily News*), *IT Business* and a host of others. In Information Technology departments, big and small, across the country, these publications were how you kept up to date in a fast moving, ever evolving profession referred to by the two initials—'IT.'

As a great marketing feature, you had to qualify for a subscription based on these publications' criteria as being a purchaser or influencer of technology purchases and adoptions. If you held one of the coveted work titles of CIO, Director or Manager you showed your status by having the publication with your name on the label, conspicuously displayed on your desk or for those of higher rank, your office table.

Our journey into Digital Transformation

As we will repeat throughout this book, we didn't know we were embarking on a digital transformation. We thought we were fighting to save this iconic business. As such, it would be dishonest to look back with hindsight and retrofit our journey as if we had developed and followed a framework or roadmap.

Our journey began in the early stages of what has come to be known as Digital Transformation or by the agonizingly unintuitive initials—DX. There was precious little to guide us except perhaps for the few almost mythological stories that were the stock and trade of speakers at industry forums.

Even these were problematic. Any first-hand account of a current business story must be questioned in terms of its objectivity. If the person is still with a public company, there are often limits on what they can say. If they have left the company, one may wonder if that has coloured their opinions.

What we have found lacking is a frank discussion about problems and issues, at a sufficient level of detail that captures the experience not just of companies, but of the people who lead and live through those changes.

A first-person account

All of this led us to the idea of a 'first-person story' which is as objective as we are capable of telling. In this regard, we perhaps had some advantage over other authors. Both of us have achieved that rare commodity that the late David Broadfoot used as the title for his last comic tour. We are "Old Enough to Say What I Think." We also have the added benefit of being the majority shareholders in a private company which allows us another degree of freedom. We have, of course, brought our own experiences and viewpoints to this project.

Fawn Annan, MBA, president and CEO of ITWC (IT World Canada) has had a long career in the industry. She founded one of the largest technology trade shows of its time, the *UNIX/Open Systems* show and went on to build a *CIO Boot Camp* that led her to her first job at IT World Canada. Since that time, she has risen through the ranks, heading every area in the company and eventually being named president and now CEO.

Jim Love, FCMC, has been in IT for more than 35 years, working in operations, development and executive management roles. Jim started in financial services where he headed both IT and product areas. Partway through his career he joined Ernst & Young as a strategic consultant. He went on to head a world-wide consulting practice with DMR Group before coming to IT World Canada as CIO. In recognition of his contribution to the industry Jim was made a Fellow of the Institute of Certified Management Consultants in 2002 (FCMC).

Despite the academic leanings of both authors, this is not a book about theory. Both of us have strong academic backgrounds and value the insights that can be derived from rigorous academic investigation and analysis. Fawn has an MBA from University of Cumbria in the UK. Jim has taught at several universities in Canada and internationally. But in this book our approach is firmly rooted more in application than academia and in the practical day to day work we have been engaged in.

We will, however, where it's relevant, refer to some models and frameworks throughout this book from noted researchers such as Michael Porter and Jim Collins. Their work is powerful because it took years and in some cases decades of painstaking objective analysis to create the models and frameworks for which they have become famous. Ultimately, however, an academic analysis is retrospective. It sifts through the data created by multiple experiences and events and looks for patterns and insights from that data. By observation, reflection and analysis it finds common patterns and produces a framework for later lessons. We had no such luxury. What we were experiencing was uncharted territory. We were forced to confront the first wave of digital disruption as pioneers, often looking in vain for utility in the old models yet without new models or frameworks to guide us.

Although we present this as a 'first person' story, we have tried to achieve some degree of objectivity, while realizing, as we noted earlier, that no story is completely objective. In the end, we offer you what we discovered, what we experienced and what we learned. It is from our actual journey through digital transformation that we feel we have the most to share in what we hope will be the start of a continuing dialogue.

There is still much to learn and experience. Digital transformation is still being defined. In our opinion, it is still not fully understood or perhaps tragically misunderstood. The definitions range from the apocalyptic to the cynical.

We have all heard the apocalyptic predictions and no doubt cringed at the misinformed hysteria that they represent. Lately, in reaction to this, we have seen a spate of articles which purport to expose the apocalyptic hype surrounding 'Digital Transformation.' One recent and typical article quoted an executive with a large company involved in several large 'Digital Transformation' projects who bemoaned the fact that he didn't truly know what digital transformation was. The implication, of course, is that is some kind of a 'fad' and that companies are throwing themselves into it without real thought or understanding. That may indeed be true, but it doesn't disprove the reality of digital disruption and the need for transformation. It does show, rather unflatteringly for this executive and others who take this stance, a lack of understanding of strong management and real leadership. Leaders don't plunge their business into something they don't understand and blame peer pressure or media hype.

We have also seen articles which try to prove digital transformation is nothing new. They do this by placing it into a familiar category. It is, they say, no more than a new name for 'continuous improvement' or 'reengineering' or any of the other schools of business improvement or consulting methods from the past decades. This may be more dangerous than the hype it purports to counter. Equating digital transformation with other familiar terms can lull us into a false sense of security, if it causes us to respond to truly new challenges with old and consequently ineffective approaches. We may feel, erroneously, that we are doing something to address these new problems when all we are doing is masking the symptoms and reducing the time available to respond when the impact of disruption hits us.

One does not have to be an apocalyptic "end is nigh" prophet of doom to recognize that digital transformation, or rather the disruption which it responds to is not the 'same old, same old.' It represents nothing less than a fundamental change to every aspect of how we do business. We cannot predict the impact of disruption. What we can predict accurately is that all businesses will eventually feel that impact.

We can say with certainty that digital transformation is revolutionary, not evolutionary. It is not a new approach to continuous improvement. It is a not a trend or a fad. Many businesses have attempted to implement at least one of the many business improvement approaches that have popped up over the past decades. Undoubtedly, some of these could be beneficial, whether they were true innovations or re-workings of prior concepts. Other attempts might be seen as fads.

Regardless, the sad reality is that despite good intentions, all too many of these met with less than expected results, some even with outright failure. The difference between these and addressing digital transformation is that if you failed in the past with be it with a fad or the even a poor implementation of a great concept, the consequences were rarely fatal for the company. There were losses and issues, but most of these were forgotten over time. Companies got results, projects faded away or regardless of results, they simply 'declared a victory' and moved on.

In fact, on an individual basis, the leaders of these companies not only survived, but often thrived, regardless of outcomes. CEOs have all too often been rewarded for high profile bold adventures even if these ultimately left the shareholders and employees poorer. We've seen the bailout bonuses of Wall Street after the US financial meltdown or CEOs like BP's Bob Dudley whose compensation package totalled 19.6 million dollars when the company posted one of its largest losses. The list is extensive. The problem is well known but goes unaddressed. Nevertheless, whether the management actions led to modest gains or tragic errors, companies have survived a vast number of trends, fads and methodologies.

Digital transformation is different. It is the "open heart surgery" of organizational change. If you make a mistake, the patient dies.

For us as the new owners and investors in IT World Canada the risks were very real. If we failed, so would the company. We would lose our investment. But we weren't the only ones who would be affected. We were also responsible for the people who worked for us. Mistakes and failure would hurt more than just the two of us.

We have made mistakes, although thankfully, none have yet been fatal. We've also had some successes. We have learned a great deal, but even after the years we have spent working on our corporate transformation, we don't have all the answers. We have one, and only one absolute certainty. Digital disruption is real and has affected or will affect us all regardless of size of company or industry sector. Those who fail to recognize the threat it poses will pay a price. Those who tackle it and find opportunity in their transformation will survive and possibly thrive.

We hope that our respect for the seriousness of digital transformation, combined with what we also hope is a frank and honest first-person account will lead the you to contemplate your own situation, offering you some helpful insights to meet the challenges ahead.

In the first two sections of the book we will share our perspective and our first-hand account of our journey to date.

For those who are looking for frameworks or roadmaps, we offer a third section. In this section, we take what we've learned and try to formulate that into some tools that can be used or at least the beginnings of more analytical framework. These are not perfect, and much more can be developed, but it is much more than we had to work from. Fittingly, this third section is digital and found on a special website open to all who purchase the book. You can find it a www.dxfirstperson.com.

There is no clear ending, only a sense of beginning, a gateway to the concepts, trends and lessons learned, to help others with their own digital transformation journey.

Part I

The Age of Accelerated Innovation

We are entering an era of accelerated innovation. Over the next few years, the pace of change will increase at a rate which will make the previous decades seem slow in comparison. It may be hard to accept, but it doesn't make it any less true.

We've become desensitized to the phrase 'the pace of change' and with good reason. Many of us have lived through a vast number of 'major' changes and 'paradigm shifts.' We have seen the birth of rock and roll, the emergence of television, the Woodstock revolution, putting a human on the moon, the birth of the micro-computer, the Internet, email and e-commerce, the high-tech boom and bust, globalization and most recently the explosion of social and online media. Each of these on its own represented a revolutionary level of change.

Each brought it both promises and threats. To supporters, we entered a new and wondrous era for those who embraced the way of the future and a cataclysmic reckoning and extinction for those dinosaurs that did not leap forward into the change. To detractors, we feared the threat to our social order and our very way of life. Whether you saw the positive or negative impacts, we have all lived through at least one, or for most of us, many more periods of 'radical change.' But we have heard that phrase so many times that it has become trite and hackneyed.

Despite the promise of the brave new world on one hand or the apocalypse on the other, somehow, we survived. There were casualties and real impacts along the way. Corporate giants disappeared. Entire industries were devastated and only exist, if they still do, as shadows of their former selves.

Each wave of change has left lasting impacts. They have also influenced us in ways that we might not truly appreciate. For example, at the start of the last century the introduction of electricity had manifold impacts on our personal lives. The way we light and heat our houses, our various appliances—these and more—are the artifacts of the 'electrification' of our world.

Each wave also changed our businesses. For example, we can look at the effect that electricity had on how factories were built and even how they were run. Formerly driven by water and later steam power, factories were designed to be tall and compact, centralized around the drive shafts and pulleys that supplied their mechanical power. The introduction of electricity changed that, allowing for newer low-rise buildings as our factories moved from multi-story riverside edifices to the sprawling automated assembly lines of today's large industrial parks.

The automobile, a product of those same assembly lines, also affected every aspect of our personal and work lives, blurring the lines between personal and commercial. It changed the nature of our cities, introducing the modern sprawling suburbs. It brought on the birth of the suburbs and the decline of the intercity core. It also introduced the shopping mall, the drive-in restaurant and take-out fast food chains. Would there have been a McDonald's without the ubiquitous automobile?

The introduction of electronic computers brought with it changes to the modern office as mechanical and card-based systems were replaced by large remote mainframes and later by desktop microcomputers. Those new devices led to the introduction of 'white collar business automation' with spreadsheets as the vehicle for numbers, ledgers and even databases—all of which changed not just the way we worked, but where we worked and even the very nature of our work. Would the concept of the 'knowledge worker' be possible without the ubiquitous computer?

As far reaching and rapid as these past changes were, the pace would only continue to increase over the last century and into this one. It is difficult to believe that as late as the middle 1990's, what we know of as the World Wide Web had existed only for a few years and was accessible to very few. Even in its first decade of public existence it was little more than a new way to publish and read formatted text. Yet in a few short years it brought us e-commerce and a consumer revolution.

Given the ubiquitous nature of mobile devices and the way they have changed our business lives, it is equally amazing to reflect that BlackBerry launched its first smart phones in 2003 and the era of consumer mobility, in effect, only really began with the iPhone launch in 2007. The mobile phone, more than any other device, has obliterated even the blurred line between personal and commercial, affecting every aspect of our lives. As we moved from the beginning of the last century to the first decades of a new century the pace of that change continued to accelerate.

A *Harvard Business Review* article from 2013 gave a short but impactful summary of this a featuring a graph created by the *New York Times* writer Nicholas Felton. The graph shows the speed of adoption of technology from telephone to cellphone.

Michael DeGusta of *MIT's Technology Review*, commenting on Felton's analysis, noted how each successive wave of change accelerated in terms of adoption time:

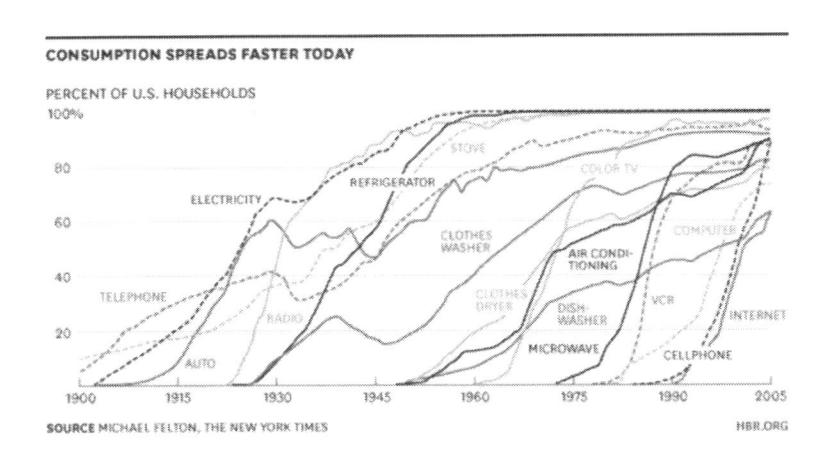

Source: https://hbr.org/2013/11/the-pace-of-technology-adoption-is-speeding-up

"It took 30 years for electricity and 25 years for telephones to reach 10% adoption but less than 5 years for tablet devices to achieve the 10% rate. It took an additional 39 years for telephones to reach 40% penetration and another 15 before they became ubiquitous. Smart phones, on the other hand, accomplished a 40% penetration rate in just 10 years, if we time the first smart phone's introduction from the 2002 shipment of the first BlackBerry that could make phone calls and the first Palm-OS-powered Treo model."

Each of these waves of change had a profound impact on industries, places, towns and, of course, on people. Every aspect of our companies including our jobs, the way we live, work and play—even our relationships—our entire social fabric was fundamentally altered with each successive wave of technological adoption. The changes have been so far-reaching that it is said that over the last century the world has been unrecognizable and perhaps even unimaginable to each successive generation.

There is an old saying that "a recession is when your neighbour loses her job and a depression is when you lose your job." So it was with the changes over the last hundred years. Technology changed our lives. There were upheavals, wins and losses. In a business sense, everyone felt some degree of change, but how or how severely you were impacted depended on the time, the change and the group or sector of the workforce that you were in. There were changes in work and in the workforce. Some were easier to adapt to; some were severe in their impact. Some people lost their jobs, others got iPhones. Overall, life moved on.

At the start of the 21st century, the expansion of the Internet, micro-computers and the early phases of digitalization took change to a new level with seismic shifts and displacements that were more rapid and much broader in their impact, affecting a wider range of industries and companies.

But this time it was different. In the last century, the automobile rapidly replaced the horse and buggy but didn't immediately wipe out the underlying manufacturing industry itself. Wagon makers became the first automakers, adapting their facilities to manufacture the new vehicles and mastering the mechanics of the internal combustion engine. The new 'horseless carriage, at least in its first decades was still primarily still a carriage, albeit with a different engine. It took many decades for the industry to consolidate as individual companies were gradually bought out by the growing automotive giants.

In stunning contrast, the new digital revolution wiped out entire industries and segments of industries not over decades, but in a matter of a few years. As one example, almost none of us use them today, but as little as ten years ago, 'travel agent' was a real job paying decent wages. The travel agent had a busy job, serving customers with flight bookings, hotel reservations, right down to booking rental cars and entertainment venues for vacationers, but overwhelmingly for business customers.

By 2010, in only a few short years, new services on the Internet wiped out this part of the travel industry. In the UK over 75,000 travel agents lost their employment in a matter of only a few years. In North America and the rest of the world the situation was identical. The few travel agents who remain are a tiny fraction of the industry who have found some niche that allows them to survive—at least for now.

In recent times, technological change has occurred more rapidly and with greater impact. Companies and even entire industry sectors have been decimated or virtually wiped out in years, not decades. Gone is the concept of change as long powerful waves. These new changes seemed more like brush fires, burning hot and fast and devastating everything in their path.

The first to fall were the industries where the products were easily digitized. Not only travel agencies disappeared. The encyclopedia industry was wiped out. Record and books stores disappeared. The replacement of film and development by digital photography destroyed the industry and took with it one of the world's most iconic brands—Kodak.

The ultimate irony is that Kodak invented the digital camera. Its own studies had predicted that digital photography would ultimately prevail. But few, if any, saw how fast digital photography would eliminate film. The numbers involved are staggering. In 1988, Kodak employed over 140,000 workers. Today the shell of the company that has emerged from bankruptcy employs approximately 6,000 workers. The 134,000 lost jobs, as shocking as it is, does not tell the full story. It does not count all the related companies that did photographic development and processing around the world. Nor does it include the manufacturers of the equipment and chemicals that drove this industry. When the former 'blue chip' company fell, the impact was as severe as it was swift. The industrial equivalent of a medium sized city simply disappeared in a few short years.

While these industries were the first victims, others were also vulnerable. The hollowing out of U.S. manufacturing had been in progress for years. Automation and globalization devastated North America including the U.S. Midwest and parts of Canada. Tens of thousands of high paying, often unionized jobs, moved offshore in a very few years while the distribution and management end of the supply chain was controlled by relatively few employees.

Wage arbitrage—the vastly lower wages in the developing world—was certainly a key factor in the movement of industrial and manufacturing jobs out of the U.S. and Canadian economies. But it was truly the new micro-computers and digital communication that enabled globalization to become such a powerful force. Supply chains spanned the globe and were run by computer software. The physical work of manufacturing and later even highly skilled work like computer programming and other tasks were performed offshore but managed onshore by local knowledge workers and digitally enabled management.

Companies who were vulnerable felt the impact rapidly. They tried to make changes to meet the new world reality, but many could not move fast enough. By the time Kodak tried to shift into new lines of digital cameras, the separate consumer level camera was moving towards extinction.

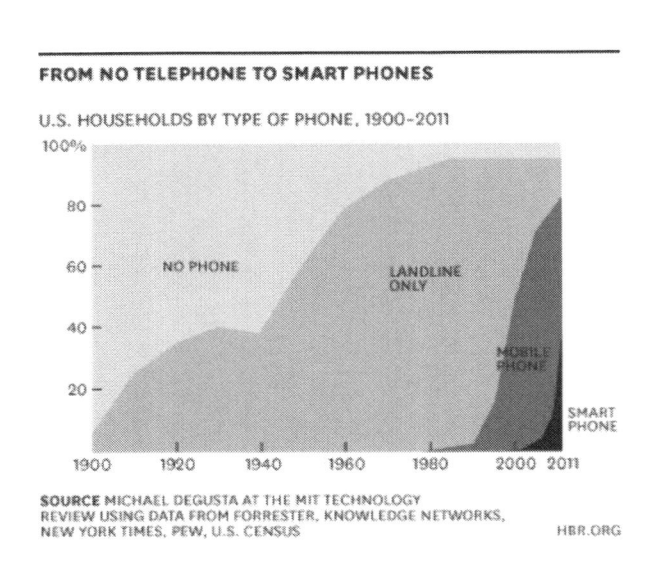

FROM NO TELEPHONE TO SMART PHONES

U.S. HOUSEHOLDS BY TYPE OF PHONE, 1900-2011

SOURCE MICHAEL DEGUSTA AT THE MIT TECHNOLOGY REVIEW USING DATA FROM FORRESTER, KNOWLEDGE NETWORKS, NEW YORK TIMES, PEW, U.S. CENSUS   HBR.ORG

The smartphone, developed in North America but manufactured overseas, was the final nail in the coffin for the consumer camera, which itself had only been a serious competitor to film for less than a decade. It was only a matter of a few years after the launch of Apple's iPhone before the mobile phone eliminated the need for a separate digital camera. Given the speed at which this occurred, Kodak had no possible pivot and succumbed to the forces of digital disruption. The company went into bankruptcy with its only remaining assets being its patents, ironically, some of these for inventions in digital photography.

As fast as the market penetration of the smart phone might seem, we have not yet reached the limits of the speed of adoption for a new technology. Each successive wave converges with and builds on the foundations established by the prior changes and innovations while the pace of adoption continues to accelerate to levels that become almost impossible to comprehend.

For example, augmented reality has been with us for several years. It has interesting possibilities, some applications, but in the mainstream, it did not yet have wide usage. Then came *Pokémon Go*.

The convergence of smart phones, embedded cameras and the powerful digital networks that carriers implemented to serve consumer demand for photo sharing, when brought together, created a platform enabling a technological development like augmented reality to achieve global penetration in under a month. The card game that led to *Pokémon Go* had an audience, but when it migrated to a mobile format it took augmented reality with it to an enormous market penetration. From an almost 'cold start' in May of 2018 it had 147 million users worldwide and over a billion downloads within a month.

In terms of market penetration, the sheer numbers were astonishing. But there was another development, itself of epic proportions. It turns out that a significant number of *Pokémon Go* players (43%) were female. It had not only broken records for rapid market penetration, but also it simultaneously tapped into and captured a new and previously underdeveloped market segment at the same time and with the same speed.

Which brings us to the present day where, as impossible as it might seem, most industry and social analysts believe that we have not yet seen the full impact of digital transformation. Many believe that the next decade will usher in truly massive changes that will affect every business regardless of size or industry. We are about to experience what one analyst from research firm IDC called 'the era of accelerated innovation.' All industries, companies, economies and our entire society will feel the full impact of digital disruption at a rate and with an impact that will make the past decades pale in comparison.

The previous waves of change have indeed had enormous impacts, but there were limitations that regulated the speed at which they could move. Each built on prior technological innovations, but largely in an evolutionary pattern and somewhat sequentially. What would happen if the limitations were removed? What if several prior changes converged so that change happens not at the pace of the landline telephone or even the smartphone but at the pace of *Pokémon Go*? What if these rapid changes were no longer restricted to digital products or services but could now encompass any product or service in any industry?

There are valid reasons to think that this is indeed what is about to happen. The trend towards acceleration continues. On their own, each technological innovation has an impact, but when several factors converge to create the tinder, the spark of a new digital technology burns fast and bright. At the same time firms are struggling to react quickly enough to survive in this changing market. Previously, affected companies and industries could not move fast enough when the impact was spread over a decade or more. How will the next wave cope when change is measured in months or even days?

How will we describe a future where entire industries are wiped out in the blink of a digital eye? What superlative will be left to describe the pace and impact of change?

This is where we are. We are at a convergence point of technical and social forces. The limits of change are being stripped away. The two fundamental laws of technological value are converging.

Many of us are familiar with Moore's Law. Named after Gordon Moore, a co-founder of Intel, the law describes how technological progress continuously doubles the power of technology. Moore's Law explains how technologies that were once affordable only by the largest companies or governments will eventually make their way into wide distribution on an even larger scale.

Although it has been declared dead many times, Moore's law has survived and if anything, increased in terms of the speed of each cycle.

There is another lesser known law, called Metcalfe's law. It was named after Robert Metcalfe, an early pioneer of the Internet and credited as the inventor of Ethernet upon which all Internet networking was based. Metcalfe's law predicts the exponential growth in the value of networks. Rather than a simple numeric doubling, powerful as that is, Metcalfe predicted that a network grows in value *exponentially*, by the square of its 'nodes'—the participants in the network.

Each of these laws independently predict massive growth and acceleration. One features increased computing power at less *cost* and the other the increased the *value* of a network. The two laws are about to, or may have already converged, and the impact is inestimable. Mobile technology, social networks and the ever-increasing speed and power of a cloud enabled technology platform now combine to allow things to happen that were never before possible. Enabling a company to take a new technology-based offering to a high level of market penetration in days rather than years is the new reality.

For years, the Internet has disrupted and even destroyed businesses and at the same time, created entirely new companies and even industries. These first disruptions were relatively easy to predict, as the end products lent themselves to becoming digitized. Music, publications and even photography were disrupted. We saw the first Darwinian massacres of the digital revolution. The rest of the promised Internet revolution stalled, however, as the abilities of this new technology were still somewhat limited. The result was that the bubble of expectations burst around 2003, and many of what might have been the new titans of industry either failed or went into a new era of consolidation.

Despite the limitations of this first wave, the carnage was felt, even by industry giants. The music industry, which had long controlled all music creation and distribution felt the one-two punch of piracy and easy distribution as perfect digital copies and download over the Internet broke their monopoly. Digital cameras embedded in consumer phones developed into high resolution cameras and digital video recorders that rivalled professional equipment. This took down Kodak, Polaroid and a host of others who manufactured cameras, camcorders and all the associated products and services that those devices required. When digital photography and video found wide distribution on the Internet it also enabled the emerging social media platforms and shook first the entertainment and then news industries to their core. Content creation and information publication of all kinds became democratized. More and more the consumer was an active and valuable participant—not just an observer.

The fundamental laws of business and even economics we had learned in university, business school and in our work experience were being challenged, transformed and rewritten. Mass production, automation, outsourcing and even globalization had made an impact on business and industries, yet none of these totally broke the existing business models by making changes at the most fundamental level.

For example, Michael Porter's famous five forces model had for years provided a framework to understand and respond to competition in a market or an industry. Porter's model showed how to survive in a competitive environment by dealing with five central forces.

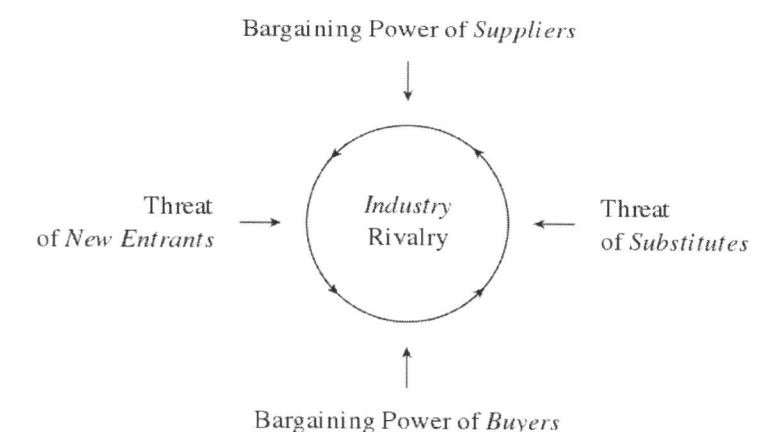

```
              Bargaining Power of Suppliers
                           ↓
                      ╱─────────╲
   Threat      →    │  Industry  │   ←    Threat
of New Entrants      │   Rivalry  │       of Substitutes
                      ╲─────────╱
                           ↑
              Bargaining Power of Buyers
```

Source: Wikipedia "Porter's Five Forces Analysis"

At the center of Porter's model is business rivalry or competition, which he regards as a positive force. Competition makes companies stronger. The other four areas are comprised of two sets of powers and threats that need to be managed. The power of your suppliers and customers must be controlled and kept in some sort of balance. Equally, you must manage the threats posed by new entrants and substitute products.

When faced with a change in a competitive force, for example, the emergence of outsourcing as a threat, large companies found strategies to continue to manage or control its effect. In the case of outsourcing, many simply embraced it to drive down their costs and remain competitive. When market tastes changed and new customer segments evolved, they had new preferences. Companies identified these with their market research and addressed them by pivoting and shifting their products and marketing strategies. There were a few disasters, such as the failure of New Coke, but overall, companies adapted.

Porter's Five Forces explained it all with a model that is at first glance simple, yet ultimately elegant and extremely powerful. True to Porter's claim, it had much more depth and precision than the more general SWOT (Strengths, Weaknesses, Opportunities and Threats) model he sought to replace.

Yet even Porter's model breaks down in the current day, although not because the type or number of forces has changed. It's less useful because the forces attack with such a devastating impact and speed, such a radical departure from the current business model, that an organization may not be able to have time or even the ability to 'manage' them. It is one thing for a competitor to find a way to radically drop their cost of production as they did with outsourcing. It's totally another thing when the cost of production and even distribution of a new unit approaches zero because they have totally reinvented the products and services and in a way that will better fulfil the customers' needs.

Porter certainly contemplated that his model would need to evolve. His inclusion of substitutions as a separate factor extended the life of this framework into the early part of the digital era. It allowed for a time where products emerged which would not compete on existing features, but would offer a substitute for their competitor's products and services. It is not certain that he contemplated a world where all five forces are so strong that they negate or disrupt the ability to react in time with any realistic strategy.

As we discuss in the chapter '*Outrun the Bear*,' the new digital enterprise exists in a world where all five of these forces attack simultaneously with no obvious line of defense. How do you deal with the power of buyers when they can move to a new company with a single click of the mouse? How do you leverage your power over supplier relationships, at an advantage, when the raw materials of your product are electrons? How do you defend against the power of substitution when the substitution is not an inferior copy, but fundamentally a truly better alternative for at least a segment of our client base?

It turns out that these questions, powerful as they might be, were only the first salvo of the digital revolution. Today, there are new questions. What defensive strategy can you mount against new entrants when the barrier to entry for a global competitor is whether or not they have a credit card? That's literally what has happened as new cloud infrastructures, global networks and Software as a Service (SaaS) applications allow a new company to set up, have a full infrastructure and start business in days or even hours—often with an outsourced production that can be paid for only when there is a sale. Suddenly, all the assets of a legacy company and the power that these once had as barriers to entry are negated.

Even the central tenet of Porter's model which says that rivalry is critical to keeping us on our toes is challenged when that rivalry becomes hyper-competition. In hyper-competition, by the time you recognize the competitive threat it can be too late for a legacy organization to respond.

Even if current models can explain what is happening, we are operating in the extremes with conditions that only existed in a classroom or textbook. Economists have spoken about 'perfect competition' but that occurred in a theoretical world inside the lecture hall, not the real world of business populated by companies with actual assets of production and run by human beings with real payrolls, expenses and investors to satisfy.

The failure of the old business models may not be that they are inaccurate, but that they presume a world where the old rules still apply. They foresee timeframes for response where there is time for study and analysis and measured strategic response are possible. That is a trap.

If we only see the world through a lens which assumes past conditions still apply, we are doomed to remain 'legacy companies', playing by the old rules. Faced with aggressive digital competition, companies will fail if their management believes their ability to retain their customer base is protected by some fictional 'legacy armour,' and they don't need radical change. It is a mistake to believe that the old strategies will provide a barrier to entry that will effectively block a new digitally enabled competitor.

When a new competitor refuses to play by the rules, legacy companies are hugely vulnerable. For example, when that new competitor selects only the market segment that is most profitable and easiest to woo, even smaller digitally enabled competitors inflict damage disproportionate to their size. When they invent a totally new way of meeting the needs of the customer and creating an unmatchable customer experience, the legacy company is suddenly challenged and devastated by this unexpected and powerful new competitor.

Some companies won't see the changes in time to react because of another erroneous assumption. They follow a mistaken belief that the next wave of digital competition will be like the first. They think that a digital product is the only end state of digital transformation. Such thinking leads to the faulty and disastrous conclusion that for an industry to be disrupted, the product or service must be able to be rendered in a digital form. Nothing could be further from the truth.

That misconception was reinforced by early industry gurus who spoke of this digital revolution as a movement from 'atoms to bits,' i.e. from physical to digital. While it's a great metaphor, it creates the illusion that an industry cannot be disrupted if its products cannot be rendered in a digital form. This leads to a sense of complacency that keeps organizations from taking action before the impact of a disruptive competitor decimates them or their industry.

The taxi industry believed it could not be digitally disrupted until someone invented something like a Star Trek transporter. The hotel industry likewise believed that their large investments in real estate presented an effective barrier to entry from a new competitor. Those misconceptions and the sense of complacency they foster are in large part why new digital competition such as Uber and Airbnb took these industries by surprise. It's why the devastation that they brought was so swift and damaging.

Even those who see change coming eventually may be lulled into complacency. They may think they have more time than they actually do. Without a sense of the speed of the impending threat, or an understanding that the new competition need not address all customers or even have a fully mature product, they are not able to see the damage that can be done when a competitor leverages even a partial or rudimentary digital enablement supported by a creative business model.

An early incarnation which illustrates this is the 'Wizard of Oz' model first used by Amazon in its early book retailing. Amazon presented itself with a digital front end that was exciting and innovative. Behind the scenes, however, the picture was starkly different. The company had distinct manual processes carefully masked from the end customer. Jeff Bezos talked about one of the early innovations being a better table for sorting and loading boxes for shipping. It was sorely needed when the initial handful of Amazon employees gathered at night after their day jobs to print and pack orders for their fast-growing bookselling site. Initially, book retailers failed to take this new threat seriously. That, it turns out, was a fatal mistake.

In this new world, companies can come to market with an exceptional product even if they are missing essential elements, if their products or services are sufficiently compelling in terms of the customer experience. Customers, at least initially, are willing to accept some limitations in return for other significant improvements in their overall experience.

The original iPhone was dismissed by many business users because it lacked some very basic productivity functions like 'cut and paste.' Despite these flaws, it overwhelmed the more functional BlackBerry, not because the iPhone was a digital product but because it was a gateway to the digital world, with an amazing customer experience. Its intuitive interface, packed in a compact and beautiful design, appealed not to logic but to emotion. It was not a product. It was an 'experience.'

The real threat is not the digitization of the end-product. The real and present danger occurs when any aspect of production can be reconceived through a digital lens, and in a way that breaks it free of the limitations and encumbrance of legacy systems and processes. When this occurs, it's not the product, it's the experience and the business model itself that undergo a fundamental change. That change, combined with other factors that extend its reach or make costs more elastic, such as the gig economy, social media or others, results in numerous devastating competitive blows all happening at the same time. The end cost of production or distributing a new product or service may not fall to zero, it may not be 'atoms to bits,' but it can still be a quantum level ahead of existing legacy competitors. It presents a competitive threat that legacy companies cannot match.

These new competitors do not play by the old rules. Not only can they isolate only a segment of the legacy companies' business or may not need to have an initial scale. They may not even have to have financial targets for profitability for many, many years. These companies can and do effectively substitute growth for profitability. Salesforce.com is a great example of a company that grew sales year-over-year, becoming the leader in Customer Relationship Management (CRM) software without achieving profitability. It has been around since 2002, yet as late as 2016 was still losing money. Digital disruptors do not even have to obey the rules of market economics that govern and often punish even minor violations by their legacy rivals.

When you marry these advantages with an offering that meets a previously unmet and even unspoken aspect of the customer experience, these new competitors wreak havoc in the market and catch their larger competitors by surprise.

These factors reverse the very idea of barriers to entry. They keep the legacy market leader from exercising any strategy to control the forces that are now turned against the incumbent. New entrants turn these same forces against their legacy rivals and keep them from pivoting or transitioning quickly enough to match the accelerated speed of their new competitor's market penetration.

In these circumstances, even proven past frameworks like the Five Forces model either don't work anymore or blind us to the real situation so that companies try to react with strategies that are simply ineffective. When the rules have so fundamentally changed, models that are mired in the previous competitive environment become more than useless. They become dangerous.

Disruption is driven by forces that cannot be 'controlled' and where the new entrants act like martial artists, turning former strengths and new market forces against their legacy competitor. As we will discuss in the chapter '*The Dot-Customer*,' digital disruption not only reinvents the means of production but also fundamentally changes the customer interaction. It taps into unmet and previously unidentified needs. It channels deep frustrations with the current customer experience. It enables a world where the customer cannot be 'managed.' Any attempt to do so will be not only be futile, it will often create an angry backlash and unleash the emotional power of years, if not decades of pent-up frustrations.

Shelle Rose Charvet illustrated this in her book *The Customer is Bothering Me*. Charvet points out that when a customer has a grievance, they abhor being restricted by rules or policies. Any attempt to make them comply, however reasonable it might be, will only serve to further frustrate and anger them. The dilemma facing large legacy companies is that their strength, their control and their economy of scale stem from requiring that customers and staff follow uniform processes. Moving to a digital competitor even with an imperfect offering is not only a welcome relief but also a form of cathartic revenge on those who demand they 'follow procedures.'

The idea of the customer taking more control is not new. For years, we have seen the evolution to the where the customer is more well informed with almost total access to information. Features and price comparisons are done with ease. They know they have alternatives. Likewise, we have all heard the famous adage that the competitor is only a click away. What few appreciated was the depth of frustration that would be unleashed when customers discovered this power.

The digital revolution put the customer in total control and tapped into pent-up frustration at having been controlled by corporate marketing. Their reaction created what we call the 'dot-customer,' as predicted by the 1999 hit book *The Cluetrain Manifesto*. We have referenced this before, but a prescient line from that book poignantly expresses the deep and profound power that has been unleashed. New competitors are promising new approaches with vastly improved customer experience, and they are simultaneously defeating legacy products and services in terms of cost. That is why these words should be the core and inspiration of every digital transformation. *"We are not seats or eyeballs or end users or consumers. We are human beings—and our reach exceeds your grasp. Deal with it."*

Digital disruption is incredibly powerful not because of technology, but because it starts with the customer and totally reimagines the product, service or offering based on the creation of a vastly superior customer experience. The convergence of technology, corporate and social changes make this possible, but without that final element of customer experience the technology simply leaves an untapped potential—necessary but not sufficient to be competitive.

The desire for this new customer experience refuses to be contained or restricted by an existing legacy organization. While the new cloud technologies are often a key component, if it were only about the technology, the story of disruption would be much different. Digital disruptors are freed by the cloud to abandon the legacy baggage of existing companies. But they leave behind not just the legacy applications but all the concepts—location, processes and the culture of their legacy competitors.

Technology does play an enormous role in enabling disruption. A convergence of forces has been ushered in by what we have termed the 'new four horsemen' of cloud technology referred to by the somehow appropriate acronym - SMAC. SMAC is short for Social, Mobile, Analytics and Cloud. These four pillars have created a new technological platform, the impact of which we are still only just beginning to see. This platform has both empowered and simultaneously democratized technology, making it available to companies of any size, and in the process, has changed the way we think about products, services and even our role as customers and suppliers.

Today, these SMAC technologies have matured to a level where it is possible and practical to set up the entire infrastructure for a global company in an afternoon using a personal credit card. The cloud and its various platforms provide an accessible foundation to provide computing anywhere, anytime. In this new world, an ecosystem of 'apps for rent' provides a manufacturing and distribution capability equal to anything a major company might have in place—without any encumbering legacy systems.

In a world where networks are everything, Social and Mobile platforms allow anyone to reach their market in record time. They have simultaneously reinforced the desire for customer control and created a new standard for immediacy of response in the now social 'dot-customer.' Analytics from data collected throughout the end to end delivery of a product or service allow a deeper and more immediate insight into that customer experience. It is possible to tap into a universe of data available from social and web interactions. Using easily available tools allows micro-segmentation based on observed customer behaviour and even prediction of unexpressed desires. It allows a company of any size to become an analytical marketing powerhouse at a level previously attainable only by giants in their industry.

Where once only large companies could gather customer data and have the ability to analyze it, in the digital world even the most modest of firms can have access to terabytes of data and the ability to not just store but to process that data on demand. What once took millions of dollars and months of time is now available to anyone with a credit card. Freed of the legacy of assets, process and culture, new digital disruptors with their start-up mentality reimagine every aspect of the product or service to fulfil the desire for an exceptional customer experience.

The already impressive capabilities of these SMAC technologies will increase exponentially over the next few years. The hyperscale public cloud providers like Amazon Web Services (AWS) deliver thousands and thousands of new cloud applications and the components to assemble new systems to enable and drive these new business models and processes on a global scale. Already, every aspect of the infrastructure of a company from accounting to telephony can be purchased for a trivial investment. These are not cheap and troublesome copies of enterprise applications. They are robust and full featured, yet affordable and available to all. They are delivered on a globally scalable, high availability infrastructure.

New companies can reach new customers on the web and increasingly through social media via their mobile devices with laser precision target marketing. Even physical products can be designed, prototypes printed and later produced on demand with just in time delivery. The future will continue to bring new, inexpensive offerings in areas of analytics, automation and even Artificial Intelligence (AI) and inexpensive robotic manufacturing.

Ubiquitous low-cost technology is already delivered free of the restrictions of legacy corporate processes and cultures.

Technology was once adopted, explored and developed at a measured pace by large corporations, primarily due to cost. The new wave moves in the opposite direction. Consumer technology is being pushed *into* the corporation by passionate groups of devotees who may often have personal or home technology that exceeds the systems they have at work.

Recently, a speaker at a conference on Digital Transformation remarked, "why do I have Star Trek at home and the Flintstones at work?" This comment says it all. Not only customers, but the best employees are also demanding and getting new, sophisticated and always mobile technologies. The true democratization of technology has arrived.

Today, we are truly at a point in our history where technology is no longer a limitation. Increasingly, capital investment and market scale are no longer limitations. We are limited only by our imagination. Our new restriction is not our legacy systems. It is legacy processes and legacy thinking. It is our inability to jettison these old ways of thinking.

We do not trivialize this point. It is hard to abandon rules, models and years of experience by industry leaders and experts. One should not do this lightly. Those of us who inherit the task of transforming legacy companies have a foot in both worlds. We cannot simply ignore the past. Equally, however, we must recognize that predicting the future from the past is only valid if the future is fundamentally the *same* as the past, which clearly, it is not.

In the old world, our expertise was our advantage. In a world where the future plays by new and different rules, our expertise is our enemy. We have to realize that the design of past models and frameworks met the needs of their time and context. They were created by people of that time, not given to us by the divinity. They are not immortal, nor are they based on fundamental truths. They have value only as long as they offer utility. They must constantly be questioned and tested.

The paradoxical prison of past success

The prison of expertise is a key threat to existing companies—even market leaders. We've seen this firsthand. When a digital competitor emerges, it's difficult to see them coming. Even when you do see them looming on the horizon, it's difficult and sometimes impossible to react effectively.

That difficulty rises out of this paradox. To truly mount an effective competitive defense, you must compete with or even disrupt *your own* products or services. That sounds marvelous in theory. It makes a great slogan to pepper the speech of an industry guru. Looked at in in the cold light of day-to-day reality, it is something else entirely.

To properly prepare your organization for digital transformation, you must propose that your company invest money, not to *grow* sales but to make them *decline* in your current offerings, perhaps even the core or flagship products and services. You are asking for investment in a new product or service where the margins and even the market demand are unproven. As we'll discover when we look later at the new economics of digital transformation in the chapter *'Outrun the Bear'* these margins, if carefully analyzed, are inevitably lower than the current product or service margins.

Your new internal competitor will inevitably be fiercely resisted by those whose job it is to defend the company's existing products against competitive threats, no matter where they come from. Moreover, it will be an easy target. Tackling a new idea from within a company can be much simpler than fighting an external threat. Arguments can be directly or even informally presented to a management group whose compensation and bonuses are inevitably tied to increases and not decreases in sales of the existing products and services.

You will find that those whose careers, futures and status in the company are associated with the status quo will prove to be difficult opponents. Their job is to protect their product or service from competitors, and they will do it to the best of their ability. Various means of internal resistance, even sabotage, can and often will be employed. Whether you consider it the 'corporate immune system' or 'friendly fire'—the danger and risks of presenting a new disruptive idea is very real. Your own career could be negatively affected by doing what is right for the company.

Strategies of resistance are often very successful in thwarting the emergence of new and radically different offerings. It may help to explain why Kodak, whose own internal analysis clearly showed they had ten years to deal with the threat of the digital camera did nothing until it was far too late to respond.

Moving to meet a new digital competitor doesn't only require eliminating costs and friction in the current delivery model, it also requires sacrificing revenue from your prime and often currently profitable business with a hope that this will position the company in an uncertain future. That level of uncertainty explains why defending digital transformation requires a level of corporate courage that is often missing in those who have come to power on the strength of the existing products and services.

Legacy companies are dominated by quarterly revenue and earnings. For a public company, being under predictions by even as little as cent per share in earnings can generate a huge downward swing in share price. Exceeding predictions by several cents or more can have surprisingly little results. Investors and markets reward consistency and predictability far more than they reward innovation.

Even private businesses may find a meeting with their shareholders or banker is difficult when they announce that they are planning to sacrifice sure revenue for a response to an emerging but not yet proven digital threat.

New digital competitors are not bound by the same restrictions. The result is what we have termed 'uberization.' It is where a new competitor builds up the momentum to roll over an existing business or even industry sector while 'hiding in plain sight.' Even while the world watches, legacy companies fail to see and respond to the threat. When it does hit, they seem unable to respond.

From the early days of Uber there is an iconic quote, supposedly from a taxi driver who said, "when they invent teleportation, that's when I'll worry about a replacement for taxis." At this point, looking back, we can all laugh at the naïveté of this comment with smug satisfaction, as we did when we read statements from the early computer era.

The CEO of IBM once stated that the world would have room for maybe five computers. There's a list of other memorable quotes, from leaders in the industry ranging from Bill Gates' famous claim that no one would need more than 64k of memory to the founder of Digital Equipment Corporation dismissing the idea of the home computer. It is, however, not just industry leaders who are blind to the dangers of new technology. We forget that most male executives dismissed the first microcomputers simply as tools for the secretarial pool.

Humans are good at seeing major change only in retrospect. We are not as effective when we are the subjects, or when we are in the middle of that major change.

A legacy organization is unable to see and respond to change because of its attachment to its existing investments and the faith of its management, employees and investors in the current organization. It is a prisoner of its own success—its own assets. Such assets need not be physical assets. Intangibles such as processes, expertise, knowledge and ultimately culture are equal and often even more formidable barriers to change.

Expertise and knowledge are based on established rules—of the industry, of the markets, of customers or of the economy. Digital disruption doesn't have to play by those rules. That's what so hard for us to grasp and difficult to imagine. Who could predict a world where a totally new competitor would leverage digital infrastructure, social media, and the gig economy to create a taxi company that owned no taxis? Who of classic business school training would predict the success of this new competitor given that it could be more expensive than the taxi alternative it disrupted? Which sane economist would predict the emergence of a global competitor that could achieve all of this and be a decade away from making a profit?

As we've earlier noted your new digital competitor doesn't have to scale to serve all customers. They just need to take even a portion of the most profitable business. In fact, they may hope that you, their victim, will try and even succeed in holding on to the existing and often unprofitable customers. As their legacy competitors strangle themselves with their aging infrastructure, systems and old rules of commerce the new entrants are free to serve and invest to serve only the most profitable segments.

The expertise that served the legacy company so well will now serve only to confound and paralyze. What has worked before is now ineffective. The new world of digital disruption—predicted by Moore and Metcalfe, built on SMAC and following the new rules of commerce—leads us into a world where the old rules simply do not apply. If the competition doesn't play by the rules, all the heirloom expertise and knowledge, be it frameworks, models or strategies, now make a legacy business more vulnerable and less able to respond to the threat it is facing.

The era of accelerated innovation

To this point we've presented a picture of tremendous change at an ever-increasing pace. We've shown that the threat to our legacy organizations defies prior rules, models and strategies. We've noted that no industry is immune. Our final thought is— this is just the beginning. The true impact of the era of accelerated innovation has not yet arrived

Given the interest in digital transformation, with many companies acknowledging that it is actively affecting them today or will in the very near future, digital disruption is nowhere near its peak in activity or in impact. Even for those who have been battered and beaten, the knockout punch has yet to be delivered.

Industry experts from IDC, a firm that specializes in spending forecasts, predict that spending on digital transformation will grow 16.6 percent over the next five years from $1.07 trillion in 2018 to a staggering $1.97 trillion in 2022. To put it in perspective, this is three times the growth rate of general IT spending. For those who believe that the best rule of predicting corporate behaviour is 'follow the money' this surge in spending is a clear indication that digital transformation is accelerating and any peak has yet to arrive.

The acceleration will continue to be fueled by a combination of new factors that will serve as a catalyst, accelerating change beyond anything we've seen to date and perhaps anything we can imagine. This 'uberization' steamroller—a business model transformation driven by powerful and unmet needs in the customer experience—will affect every product and service in every industry and company.

In chemistry, a catalyst is something that accelerates a chemical reaction. Hydrogen and oxygen will eventually form water, but add a little palladium, and this process accelerates dramatically. An alternative and much more potent catalytic process would occur if you introduced a single spark into the oxygen and hydrogen. That will instantaneously combine these atoms to produce water. Of course, it will also produce a powerful explosion.

Current technical developments—SMAC and others—have operated at the level of palladium. They are a catalytic force. They combine with other forces to allow new companies to accelerate and surpass their legacy competitors. As surely as the ubiquitous use of mobile apps combined with the gig economy accelerated Uber's development, future developments like 3D printing will serve to accelerate a revolution in manufacturing. The twins of augmented and virtual reality will accelerate change in industries from retail to medicine. The Internet of Things (IoT) and the intelligent devices that populate our world are enabling radical changes to many industries. Robotics, with its cheap and unsleeping devices have already automated warehouses and factories and will soon move to everything from construction to restaurants. There will be more new use cases developed and brought to life as technology and innovation move forward. As they grow and combine, the steamroller effect will continue.

But the spark, the explosive catalyst, will come from Artificial Intelligence (AI). AI offers the final element to supercharge the move to a true digital enterprise with explosive growth and casualties for the bystanders.

It started as a novelty. It has been the subject of science fiction novels. It's been over-promoted, over-hyped and debunked. Yet as we sit today, AI is about to usher in extraordinary and unparalleled changes to our companies, our industries, our world and our lives.

AI replaces the one remaining limitation to the speed of change and implementation—the human factor. From its early incarnations, the idea of AI surpassing human capability made it a novelty and the darling of science fiction stories. Who could forget the lifelike speech of the HAL 2000 in the movie 2001? Today, where the voices of Siri and Alexa fill our lives, we can quibble with Arthur C. Clarke's timing, but not his predictions. The voice activated computerized intelligence is more than just the product of a clever imagination. It is an inevitability.

Even lacking the pseudo consciousness of 2001's HAL supercomputer, AI has proven itself as it moved from academia or research to the world of business. First, AI won chess championships. Years later, IBM's Watson beat a human playing the famous game show Jeopardy and demonstrating a new ability to handle imprecise information in contextual settings. Recently the world's GO champion was defeated by AI. GO has more possible variations in strategy than there are stars in the known universe. The capacity of AI to approximate cognition, to learn and execute on complex models, data and strategies is now unquestioned.

AI transcends the algorithmic approach to computing which has both dominated and limited our progress to date. Formerly, computers would store and process enormous amounts of data, and could do this in split seconds. In our old algorithmic world this could only be done based on predefined rules. It still required humans to develop and continually advance the algorithms.

Today, AI doesn't just process, it also learns—even about things which are imprecise or contextually dependent. It no longer needs humans to write algorithms, now treating these like the computer programming equivalent of GO strategies. It can make its own strategies and contextual decisions based on learning in ways that exceed the capacity of humans. AI can, for example, already learn to a point where it can diagnose certain forms of cancer with far greater accuracy than the most effective human diagnostician. With advances in wireless networks, it will not only be able to develop these strategies, but it will be able to operate in the physical world using remote machinery and devices. It will absorb billions and trillions of inputs. It will spot anomalies, find new patterns, evaluate alternatives—and act.

AI provides the brain to operate the digital business. It makes it possible to digitize enterprises in new ways and at an accelerated pace. Self-driving trucks can deliver our goods. Robots can perform the physical tasks once relegated to humans. Automated restaurants can cook to order. AI driven doctors will not only analyze and diagnose, they will even perform remote surgery with greater speed and accuracy than current physicians. We already can see all of this in action. Bringing these use cases and even more we have not yet imagined into real life use is only a matter of time.

AI will be the catalyst that enables a host of new technologies, each revolutionary in its own right. AI will do work formerly possible only by using human senses and cognitive reasoning but operating far beyond the capacity of the human mind. It will do this tirelessly, accomplishing millions of tasks in less than the blink of an eye. AI will do this in the context of a world where infrastructure and computing power is ubiquitous and cheap to run, store and process vast data sets.

Not only will AI perform at levels not possible for humans, it will adapt far more quickly. It learns new patterns at the speed of modern computer processors. It does this without the additional time required to break existing habits and build new ones that is required when we train human experts. It does not need to believe what it is doing. It offers no conceptual or cultural resistance. It needs no rationalization. It only requires data. It supports the almost instantaneous adoption curve necessary to enable global propagation of ideas or processes at speeds that make *Pokémon Go* seem slow by comparison.

There are some impediments to AI's onslaught, but these are being eliminated. For AI to power a vast array of physical devices, robotics and autonomous vehicles, remote surgical or other precision operations, the capacity and latency of our wireless networks must be eliminated. Over the next three to five years that will happen with the introduction of so called 5G networks. Current mobile networks issue and receive instructions in about 50 milliseconds, six times faster than the blink of the human eye. 5G will bring this down to an impossible 1 millisecond—fifty times as fast as our current networks. It will allow the introduction of low power and low-cost sensors and be able to take in enormous input without being swamped by the volume of signals and devices.

The remaining resistance to AI, concerns over the ethical and moral issues will inevitably fall in the face of economic and competitive pressure. If the west is reticent, China is not. China is training millions of students in AI sciences and development and will implement both 5G and AI relentlessly over the next three to five years. The economies of the west must and will respond.

All of this will happen over the next few years. How long it will take is not certain. What we do know is that, based on the adoption curves we have seen, it will be faster than we can imagine. All the technology we have referred to is currently working today in the field. Yet, as little as three to five years the AI systems we have today will seem as quaint as the dial-in modem. Leveraging the potential of this explosive catalyst, businesses of today—large and small—will be transformed or replaced by their new digitally enabled equivalents with new business models and a hypercompetitive marketplace operating at a new velocity. This new world will spawn ideas and changes that we have not yet imagined.

How will you prepare for that change? How will your business survive and prosper as we enter this new era of accelerated innovation? As tempting as it may be to think that you are helpless in the face of all this, we need to be reminded of the quote often attributed to Albert Einstein, "The best way to predict the future is to invent it."

How can you invent your own future? How can you survive and even thrive in an era of digital transformation and accelerated innovation? How can you plan for a world which we can't truly imagine?

One way is to look at those who have already been disrupted, not with an academic review but from a first-hand experience. The view of digital disruption from the inside may help to spur your imagination. We didn't have a playbook, we had to invent as we moved forward. You have the benefit of our initial steps into digital transformation.

Part II

Our Story

What follows is our first-hand experience of digital transformation as seen through our eyes.

We didn't call it digital transformation at the time. We called it survival. Both of us came to the realization that the company had to change to survive. This is the story of our transformation of the company in response to the challenges as we saw them. But it is also our personal story—what we did, what we learned and how it changed us.

Although we use a collective voice for narrative purposes, it is for all intents and purposes, a first-person account and to the best of our recollection, the unvarnished tale of our journey.

Fawn Annan, President, IT World Canada

I had survived the political wars somehow and was now President. I found out sometime later that Michael had told the previous President, Andy, who was then dying, that I was the only one that could be trusted to take over the running of the company. I had by that time done almost every job in the company.

I was summoned to Andy's hospital bed in the weeks before his death so that he could coach me on what to do with the company. I still remember how strange that was. His wife Donny said that he'd only last five minutes in conversation and I wondered why I had come. But he spent more than 30 minutes with me, on his deathbed. I remember what he repeated over and over. He kept saying, "Fawn, you have to understand, my strategies would have changed given what's going on now."

I tried to just talk to him on a personal level. He kept going back to the business. That's how important it was to him. I left thinking that this was heartbreaking. A day and a half later, he died.

Shortly after that the owner promoted me to President. I knew he wanted a man to take the job, but his prime candidate left under a cloud to continue his own digital photography business.

I knew that I couldn't do this alone. I needed to build a team. On the recommendation of David Jonah, we hired a consultant – Jim Love – to help address our strategic technology issues. It turned out with the arrival of Jim; a new ally had arrived.

Jim Love, CIO, IT World Canada

As I took the subway and RT up to the IT World Canada offices, I was excited. I had been reading those publications since the late 1970's when I started my career in IT. I remember when I first qualified for my subscription because I'd been promoted to Manager and I could tick that box in the subscription form. No more borrowing from one of the managers or directors. I could have my own subscription. I'd arrived.

I was thrilled to be visiting this iconic Canadian publication. I didn't see myself as a consulting superstar, but I'd worked for huge companies—Cisco, Inco, Nortel, Royal Bank, AT&T and governments around the world. I'd run a world-wide practice for the former DMR group. I was no novice. But I was still nervous coming to Mecca.

When I decided to open my own consulting firm in 2003, I was interviewed by Computing Canada, one of IT World Canada's publications. My picture was on the front page. I still had it framed in my office. Eight years later, with a few more grey hairs, I was on my way to see where it all happened.

On my way, I realized that I was reading IT Business on my phone, not because as a consultant I was trained to do homework, but because it's what I always did when I had a few minutes to catch up. It was still a big part of my daily reading and although it wasn't mobile friendly, I had learned through the years as a 'road warrior' to make use of all travel time.

What I saw when I got there was shocking. Even then, before major staff reductions, it looked like a mix between a film set for a 1970's office movie and a ghost town. There was 'executive row' with the offices along the windows and then cubicle farms in a large 15,000 square foot office. Many of the cubicles were empty. How the mighty had fallen. No matter, I thought. I'd be here long enough to do the job they needed and move on.

Then I met Fawn Annan—and the adventure began.

We wrote this book to share that adventure, one that continues to this day. We describe ourselves, because publishing is an industry that was one of the earliest to be disrupted by technological change, as a 'canary in the coal mine' or at times as 'a voice from the future.'

It has been our hope that a story that focused on what this looked like from the inside might be useful to those who are in the middle of change or about to encounter it.

We offer this story with a caveat. We have no perfect model, no ultimate laws of the new economy to guide you. If such a thing can exist, it has yet to be written. What we do offer you is a front row seat to the change that we have witnessed, and our reflections and actions based on that experience.

Whether these have value is a judgement only you can make.

Stop the Presses!

"I remember it so clearly. My hands were shaking. I could hear my heart pounding.

I sat in the conference room with the large mahogany table in front of me, with the large boardroom chairs sitting vacant. The room was quiet and dark.

I'd been going over the numbers all weekend. It was clear. I knew what I had to say—and what I had to do. As I stared at the paper, my mind was whirling. The numbers screamed at me from the page. They told a clear and ominous story.

I kept staring at the page, as if somehow, I could will the numbers to change. Or maybe I could see something I had missed. But the numbers wouldn't change. Our future was unclear and risky. The only certainty—staying on our current path will lead to inevitable failure.

As I look back on it today, I know one thing clearly. I never, ever want to feel that way again."

- *Fawn Annan, President, IT World Canada*

The roots of IT World Canada go back to the early months of 1979. It was founded by Canadian entrepreneur Michael Atkins when he bought Page Publishing, which produced an IT magazine. It was not the first-time Atkins had wandered into a venture on the fringes of the publishing world. His chain of weekly newspapers began on a whimsical motorcycle trip where he bought a failing newspaper in Sudbury, Ontario. From there he bought more weekly newspapers and after that some specialty trade publications. In 1979, his company Laurentian Media Group, was putting out several publications aimed at participants in the computer industry. A new division was formed called Laurentian Technomedia, or LTI for those in the know.

The first website was built in 1993 and was modelled on an elevator. You got off on different floors, which represented different topics. Michael Atkins, our owner, thought it was a waste of time. While he acknowledged that this might be the future, he didn't see how we would make money in the present.

Andy White, the group publisher at the time, knew that while our revenue would continue to come from print, the website was a statement of our presence in the market—more like a business card. Ironically, by the time we stopped print, less that twenty years later, most revenue was coming from the website and related services. The print publication had become our business card.

Although there was some online advertising in those early years, we didn't put advertising on the site. We didn't think we could successfully sell advertising at that time. The site was there so that people would know we were 'in the game.'

In 2003 the company was growing rapidly. We changed the name of the company from Laurentian Technomedia to IT World Canada. By 2007 we had bought our competitors from Transcontinental, originally spawned from Plesman publications.

With that acquisition came Shane Schick, David Web, Paolo DelNibletto, Howard Solomon, and others who would go on to become technology journalism stars in Canada. When Shane came over, things quickly started to change. A young, talented and marketing savvy writer, he had a vision of the potential of our Internet presence.

Looking back now, it was a time when we were looking for what we would become. Andy White was our visionary. He knew that the business had to evolve and was prepared to try new ideas. The website and its related email database were just the first of many ideas he tested out. Andy had the patience to develop his ideas, sometimes over a period of years. For example, when one of our writers, Dan McLean, left to become a researcher at IDC, Andy waited for the opportunity to bring him back with the idea that IT World Canada would have its own research.

A few years before, Andy had the idea to build an executive division through the CIO brand, starting with licensing a telecommunications and networking trade show from IDG called ComNet. He brought in Fawn Annan to lead this area. At the same time Andy also bought what would become a pivotal asset to move the executive division forward, *The CIO Survival Camp* that Fawn had created.

Initially, Fawn didn't see the website as a big part of this new offering and was more interested in community building. Over that time, we also started Lac Carling, a forum that brought three levels of government together to move e-government forward. This also helped us to win the Showcase Ontario RFP for twelve consecutive years and produce a huge technology showcase for Canada's largest provincial government.

Lac Carling marked the emergence of online journalism. In those early days we would set up in the lobby with laptops so the reporters could file their stories. We had to walk a fine line—many of these discussions were high level government strategies and these were not for publication. Yet, the government did want to show Canada as progressive in terms of IT in government. Canada was regarded as a leader in e-government in those days. Making the journalists visible was a signal of transparency, our way of showing that we were living up to our agreement to promote without violating the confidences of the discussions. Having these journalists publishing to the Internet also made a statement about the sophistication of this event.

From the Lac Carling experience, we began to realize the importance and power of online journalism. We started building more websites. The growth was explosive. We soon had a website for every brand. But that growth, like much of what was happening on the Internet at the time, came with a hidden cost. There was no organization. Navigation was simplistic. No one could find anything. Simply stated, it was a huge mess.

We had other challenges that exacerbated these issues and even made the situation worse. Even though we were an IT publication, we had a war between IT and the business over who would control the websites. We tried finding ways to get Andy, the real authority of the time, to back efforts to bring order to the emerging chaos. With the CIO brand and site, there were attempts to leverage Andy's idea of research to try to introduce some organization. Heather Smith from Queen's University was brought in to organize a taxonomy. Some years later, we brought in a consultant, David Jonah, who took the taxonomy idea and tried to merge that with the emerging science of search engine optimization (SEO).

We continued to try new ideas with some successes and some absolute failures. We started a procurement portal aimed at streamlining government procurement. The day we presented it, nothing worked. That presentation was a turning point, although not in a positive way. We had invested a lot of money in this and had brought together everyone who was anyone in procurement in Ontario. The embarrassment of the technical failure brought some tough questions about how much we were spending and how or even if we could effectively commercialize what we were attempting to build.

Making things worse, the print side was starting to have trouble. We weren't getting the sales we needed. The U.S. was still doing well and there were a couple of countries in Europe who were flying high with print. But in Canada, our clients were, contrary to common wisdom, much more sophisticated than their U.S. counterparts. They were looking for demonstrable results from their advertising spending. They were saying that print advertising wasn't delivering the ROI they needed in Canada. The problems with print were not just a Canadian phenomenon. The U.S. print revenue had declined as well, by as much as 50%. But being much bigger than IT World Canada, there was still money to be made in the American print world.

While sales were falling, costs continued to rise. By that time, we had a considerable number of print publications. We had *Computer World, Network World, CIO, InfoWorld*, and *CIO Government Review,* to name a few of the best known. Our print bills were in the hundreds of thousands of dollars every month. We also had huge investments necessary to keep our audience database up to the standards of the time. In addition to our direct internal investments we also paid almost $250,000 per year for readership audits required by the magazine association.

These audits later turned out to be a saving grace. When Canadian Anti-Spam Legislation (CASL) came into force we had a verifiable opted-in subscription database which we had converted to email delivery. But we didn't know that at the time. All we could see were the costs rising and the revenue dropping. We couldn't see then how online sales would ever make up for the declines we were seeing on the print side.

We ended up dropping a lot of print publications, particularly the consumer publications. We tried to take PC World (the Canadian edition) online, attracting 60,000 subscribers in the first year, but we were competing with the U.S. that had 5 million or more subscribers, many of them Canadian. Given that reality, we got out of the consumer publications altogether in print and online. IT World Canada became a fully 'Business to Business' (B2B) publisher.

By the time Fawn took over as President in 2010, the company was in deep financial trouble. We were still printing, but without enough advertising to support our costs. Michael Atkins was losing faith in the company and talking about shutting it down. Having achieved the status as number one in our market, we were now on the verge of going under.

If IT World Canada were going to survive, something bold had to happen. We simply didn't have any other choice. Not that anyone was certain that the idea of eliminating print would work. It hadn't been tried anywhere. David Hill, then President of IDG Licensing, our minority shareholder, came up for a quarterly review meeting. When learning of our bold move, he said, "I can't believe you are the first of a hundred IDG companies across the globe to stop print."

Hard lessons

At first this might seem like a one of a kind story within a specific industry, hit by the emergence of the web and digital commerce. But there are some lessons to be learned which are applicable to any company experiencing a digital disruption.

While in hindsight it looks obvious, it was difficult to see trends emerging from within the company. Yet the signs were clear. Print was declining, but it still generated a lot of revenue. It was the business that everyone knew. Others in the industry, including our U.S. partners, were still making money despite the decline in sales.

Dropping print would take millions in revenue from the top line and abandon the core and the origins of a business with decades of history in favour of a new and unproven marketplace. While the status quo was not an option, a new fully digital strategy itself was not without risks and unforeseen consequences, as we would come to see over the coming years.

One reason for these risks was that the digital alternative was not ready for prime time. The market was developing rapidly but not fully understood. The tools, while measurably better than only a few years ago, were still limited in terms of delivering an experience resembling anything like print.

From a market perspective, it was the 'wild west.' Rules and norms, to the extent they existed, were not codified, many were not well understood and those that were changed frequently. The base technology of content management, audience databases and measurement was only then emerging, and what was there was difficult to use and expensive to both acquire and maintain.

The 'business and IT divide' exacerbated these external market problems. Even in this relatively small organization there were silos struggling for control.

The 'techies' kept the new web technology running but with frequent issues and down time, often with what appeared to be the electronic equivalent of bailing wire and string. Interruptions were frequent, causes were mysterious.

Despite its promise, the limitations of our Content Management System (CMS) made even simple ideas difficult. The business was looking to keep on the leading edge, but was constantly frustrated by the limitations, interruptions, delays, missed deadlines and ever-increasing costs.

In this new frontier, there was no textbook, no road map to follow. There was also, however, no shortage of opinions. We were surrounded by journalists who felt they knew a great deal about technology. There was an emerging number of consultants and would be gurus who claimed to know where the future would inevitably lead. Unfortunately, more times than not both groups were, if not wrong, not particularly helpful. There is world of difference between writing or theorizing about technology and actually making it work on a day to day basis. We had an abundance of great ideas, but they were all lacking in the 'nitty gritty' or the 'details' where, as the saying goes, the devil lives.

There was a lot of trial and error. Many times, investments made in products, services and offerings didn't make it to market. Some failed because of technical issues. Some failed because the market wasn't ready. Some were great concepts that would never work in the real world. All of them were painful and expensive.

Compounding these issues was an emerging and confusing set of economic issues. The revenue model of the Internet was not only radically different from anything known previously but was also in a constant state of flux. It became apparent that we weren't simply moving from print to digital. We were changing from an existing troubled economic model to another that was radically different, still emerging and not well understood.

It is often said that what business craves is stability. This new world of digital publishing offered only instability and uncertainty. The old rules, concepts and strategies that had built the business no longer worked, but the new rules had yet to be written.

At times like these, only gurus and fools are certain. For us, the only real certainty was that every decision would have numerous critics, skeptics and debate without clear decisions. Given the relatively poor track record of IT projects, this was to be expected. So, even when a decision seemed so obvious that there was no long-term alternative, we would still lack a clear direction.

From the traditionalists, any new change was idiotic and risky. From the true believers and gurus, no change was bold enough. The only certainty was that we continued to lose money and as a result, had less and less to invest in technological solutions.

Fairly or not, Canada is not often seen as a bold leader in any industry. Our inherent instinct for cautiousness is well known. As we noted earlier, on a visit to our office, an expert from our US partner IDG expressed surprise that Canada was so far ahead of everyone else in the world. However, what was meant as a compliment did not inspire confidence with our owner.

Having one major shareholder with a penchant to dive into the details meant that any decision, however well researched, could be questioned or overturned. Even in the face of the proven grim financial realities, if he met another B2B trade publication publisher remaining in print, conviction that print was recovering became the CEO's mantra, at least until that publication or another similar one folded or was sold for a pittance.

Shortly after we pulled the plug on print, several Scandinavian and Asia-Pacific IDG companies reported great results from their print portfolios. These countries and regions were different markets at different stages of their digital evolution, but it still called our decision to stop print into question.

Somehow, we persevered, moving later than we felt we should and yet faster than many wanted. It was only in retrospect that we would understand that moving early in our digital transformation, though incredibly difficult, was a critical reason for our ultimate survival.

You don't want to cut a product that is still yielding even slim profits, or at least some cash flow. Nor would anyone favour abandoning that for a new offering that requires a heavy investment before it even proves its ability to produce revenue streams, let alone make money. Yet, as we've now seen time and again, we had to move before we lost the ability to rebuild or we would either disappear or cede the market to new competitors. We would wonder over the next few years, and even to this day, whether we moved fast enough, not just to stop print, but to find a clear strategy for the transformation of the company.

What we do know now from observing the failure of others is that there is a point at which you cannot recover no matter what resources you throw at the problem. We were not then and are still not sure exactly where that point is. In our struggles over the past few years and even to this day, even though we have made astonishing progress in bringing the company back from the brink, we do not know if we have done enough. We only know that we did move and are still in business because in doing so, we created new digital revenue streams and processes.

Aside from that, in running the day-to-day business, little else is certain. Outside of the giants and the aptly named 'unicorns,' for the average company, there is no goal line that you cross after which everything is fine. Despite your best efforts, you continue to live in a hyper-competitive space. The best that is offered is that you survive to fight another day.

We kept thinking back to Kodak, one of the most clearly documented failures of the time. Even when film sales declined, their offering was—forgive the pun—unfocused. By the time the giant woke up it was simply too late.

We were a privately held company of modest means. Who were we to think we were smarter and faster than Kodak? Our revenues had declined, and we didn't have the deep pockets of a large multi-national or the ability to raise that kind of money. Our bankers were expressing concern. Our main shareholder was making noises about closing the business down. We were in deep trouble.

Did we take needed action fast enough? We didn't know. As much as we could kick ourselves, we weren't fully in charge. If we had announced, even as little as a few years earlier, when print was the huge majority of profitable revenue and online was minuscule, that the company needed to throw not just exploratory investment but to bet its future on the online world, no-one would have believed it. Had the new President jumped in earlier, instead of quietly observing and keeping her conclusions to herself, Fawn would probably not be president. Fortunately for the company, Fawn kept her own counsel. When the time came, the one person that did see what was happening and had the courage to act was the president.

The hard part had just begun.

Transform or Die

"I had been watching this for two years. It wasn't like I woke up one day and said, stop print. But when the decision time came, we honestly wouldn't have a company if we didn't. We would be gone."

- Fawn Annan

Shortly after we stopped print, we faced yet another in a series of existential crises where were forced to take stock of where the company was going. Initially the move out of print seemed successful. Our first digital magazines were very popular both with readers and with sponsors. But as quickly as the numbers went up for the first editions, they rapidly declined in subsequent months and along with that, client interest in investing in these new magazines also plummeted.

ITWC's new digital editions had our same high-quality editorial content with great in-depth feature articles. They cost a lot to produce. We saved money on print but still had the high costs of developing the editorial content.

Every time we'd take one step forward and then two steps back, we'd ask why we didn't spot the problem earlier. It turns out, in digital transformation, to be the archetypal question, "Why didn't they see this coming?"

When you are faced with a truly difficult challenge in business there are two stances companies take. Some acknowledge and even 'admire the problem' but take no meaningful action. This human condition has been with us for millennia and inspired Aristotle's famous quote, "the understanding moves nothing."

Others see the impact but still find a way to steadfastly defend the status quo. Mark Twain described this human capacity to ignore what we feel we cannot change when he said ironically that "denial is not a river in Egypt." Anyone who has worked in most large legacy organizations will recognize both of these reactions.

We came to the conclusion that in a corporate sense both are driven by our perception that from the inside organizations appear to be immortal—even in the face of tumultuous changes in the company, the industry or the economy. The large strategic trends are acknowledged, discussed and then forgotten as we get wrapped up in the day-to-day. There are crises and accomplishments. Customers are lost but just when you are despairing, new ones are found. People leave and we wonder how we will cope, but somehow, we do cope and new people come with fresh ideas and new insights.

Externally there are business cycles with deep recessions. On the inside of the organization numbers are made or budgets are slashed. When revenue declines, costs are cut. In today's world where companies are so lean, the only remaining expense to cut is people. It's painful, but it happens. Life moves on.

Somehow the company itself manages to survive. You lurch from crisis to crisis knowing that it's all a cycle, that eventually there will be change in fortune, an upswing in sales and profits. That is the collective experience gained from long careers in large or established companies. Individuals may come and go, but somehow the company survives the downward slide until the turnaround. Spring will follow winter.

That's why it is such a surprise to those inside the organization when, despite upturns and successes, when you follow the logical path of results, no matter what you do, the overall trend line continues to move downward. It takes a long time to realize in an established company that there are some downward spirals that may have no recovery. History does not always guarantee immortality.

Start-ups, on the other hand, constantly face their own mortality. There is only so much initial investment, only so much runway before they must take off. A lot can go wrong. The demand for their solutions is uncertain or at least unproven. They may misjudge the market or during their product development that market may change.

Those that get past these challenges do so because of their capacity to clearly see a constant existential challenge. Proactively, they are looking for the signals that tell them to rapidly turn the company in a new direction. This happens so frequently in start-ups that there is even a term for it. It's called the 'pivot.'

The pivot occurs when you see that your planned strategy or direction needs a recalibration or even a total reinvention. Those companies that successfully make the changes do so not purely on the financial trends, but mainly from insights gained from a real connection with their desired customers. They actively listen and observe the customer and prospective customers' reaction to their product or service.

Start-ups are in a constant fight against the odds to survive. Seeing the market clearly and understanding the customer is a Darwinian necessity. Those who don't make the right pivot get weeded out. Unlike established companies, start-ups are actively aware of their own mortality.

Legacy companies, on the other hand, rarely make an effective pivot. The very few times in corporate history where there has been a truly courageous decision to abandon part of the business and pursue a new direction has required a truly visionary leader with both courage and incredible political skills to sell and deliver the idea.

Jim Collins, a renowned researcher, Harvard professor and author of such classics as *'Built to Last'* documents one such story in his bestselling book *'Good to Great.'* Collins noted that even after studying thousands of companies, how difficult it had been to find examples of those that had made a pivot that resulted in lasting growth and productivity. Darwin Smith and the sale of the Kimberly Clark paper mills is one of those few, but also the most powerful success story in the book.

Smith was an unlikely hero. As Collins points out, there are a vast number of charismatic leaders who have led their organizations in change projects that ultimately failed, albeit usually after the departure of their charismatic change champion. There are, however, precious few long-term successes.

Smith was not charismatic. He didn't seek out any fame or recognition. He was focused on a single goal. He was determined to leave the company better off at the end of his tenure and well positioned for the future. Despite all obstacles, including the resistance he faced, he managed to pivot and successfully transform the company.

The pivot meant divesting of paper mills that were profitable at the time. Moreover, the history of the company was linked to these mills. Despite that, Smith somehow knew that the company had to take a different direction, abandon the mills and push forward into consumer products. Over the years, Smith was vindicated. As we know today, paper mills faced years of troubled times, shutdowns and a host of financial and environmental problems. On the other hand, the consumer products he focused on grew at a phenomenal year-over-year rate.

It's incredibly difficult even for a leader of Smith's stature and capabilities to move before a problem becomes acute. Smith made the right choices and he should be celebrated for his vision and corporate courage. But compared to Smith, the leader of a company facing digital disruption has an even greater challenge.

Smith took two established industries and picked the one with that he thought had the greater potential for growth. The customers, technologies and markets could be understood and analyzed. One only needs to look at the data objectively and follow the trends. Yet as Collins points out, even this is exceedingly rare and requires enormous courage and leadership ability.

Digital transformation requires all that and more. It has, comparatively, huge uncertainty. On the legacy side, there is data. But even if the trends in that data have negative implications, the new industry remains unproven. You aren't choosing between retaining a division or selling it to focus on another business you think has greater potential. You are choosing between the known and the unknown.

For the pioneer of digital transformation there are few answers and many questions. The technology and even the market for the new product or service is early in its development. What if that market you move to doesn't develop? What if you move and the envisioned problems of your existing legacy product don't materialize? What if the existing problems could be fixed? Isn't it better to survive with something than leap to nothing? How long can you stay with the legacy? When is the point at which you go into full meltdown and can't move?

That's the double whammy facing the digitally disrupted company. It needs to make a transformation that any company at the peak of its success would find difficult to make and sustain. The information to make the decision is imperfect, or non-existent, but the longer it waits, the less time and resources it has to make the necessary transformation. If it waits until its legacy revenue drops or goes into freefall, without a truly deep pocketed investor, or a war chest of cash—it will be unable to make the changes necessary to survive.

In Canada, BlackBerry missed its pivot and its revenue did go into free fall. It totally underestimated the iPhone. Yet the company recovered and has transformed into a software company. While this is a tribute to CEO John Chen's brilliance and operational leadership, it was only possible because the company had amassed billions in cash. Without that, no strategy, no matter how brilliant would have saved it.

Microsoft has missed a multitude of changes in its industry that would have destroyed other companies. It survived only because of its near monopoly on the operating system and its almost accidental development of the office suite of products decades earlier. It appears to finally be transforming to meet the new 'as a service' and cloud market under Satya Nadella after the disastrous leadership of Steve Balmer. But it can only do this because of its enormous cash flow an almost unparalleled market dominance primarily from its two main software offerings.

For the rest of us, the later a digital transformation is undertaken the more likely it is to fail. There is some point at which any pivot or transformation is simply not possible. We were either at that point or perilously close. We had no massive cash reserves. We did apply to some government tax funding programs to help finance our turnaround. With the help of a consultant from one of the major accounting firms we applied for anything and everything we could, but the funds would take a few years to realize. In the meantime, we could juggle expenses and raise a limited amount of capital from the new shareholders. But turning the company around would take time.

In the meantime, we had to survive. There were bills that we had to pay.

The cost of transformation

One of the heart wrenching things about any radical transformation is the human cost. It's inevitable that some people must go—either because they no longer have jobs, or they can't adapt to the new world. Those who are forced to leave suffer monetarily but also in other ways. But those who stay also feel the impact of the change. Although there is rarely any sympathy for those who manage these transformations, the reality is that it takes a toll on them as well.

If you are at any level of management, you probably have had to let someone go. It's never pleasant, but if it's for poor performance and you've done everything you feel you could do; you can justify it to yourself. But when someone has done nothing wrong, perhaps even has been tremendously loyal and hardworking, and their job or any job that meets their skills doesn't exist anymore—or when there isn't the revenue to pay them—even the toughest of us can be as devastated as the people we must terminate. No wonder we delay, sometimes longer than we should, hoping that something will turn around.

For a small company, it was terrible. We had done layoffs a year earlier and about 10 people were let go. With that and some attrition we had shrunk to 80 people. That was painful. But the worst was yet to come. In the new post-print digital world, we would shrink from 80 to 45 staff over the course of a single year.

It didn't feel good. The people who were let go suffered, but it also took a toll on those who did the dismissals, and on the entire organization.

Morale dropped. Rumours abounded. Staff were losing faith. We lost some great people who would have been invaluable in our future transformation. We had one man running the websites, originally from Nortel. He had tremendous talent. His job at IT World Canada was absolutely secure. We needed those skills more than ever. Nevertheless, he left. So did his number two person, also a tremendously talented individual. He stayed for a while but eventually left.

These were times of severe anxiety, with the highest level of stress on Fawn. She didn't feel she had any choice. Costs had to come down and people were one of the few areas where direct costs could be cut. Despite the losses, she also knew she needed a team to succeed and at least one or two key people who were grounded and strong to help her turn the ship around. One person could not do it alone. Finding those people and holding onto them in these circumstances would be a challenge.

One bright spot was that we didn't lose any writers, at least initially. They saw that the web was the place to be. That may be because they were technology writers and they saw the technology companies that were the best in the world at that time all moving towards the web. Even from this group, however, we would eventually have to make some sacrifices.

Peter Drucker once said that the "best and the brightest are volunteers." What he meant is that the best people have alternatives. We needed to hold onto the best we had and attract a select few top additions to the team. To do this during a contraction, we had to find ways to share a vision of future success. After the second wave of layoffs in any company, no-one believes you when you say that this is the last, even if you are foolish enough to do so. So how did we encourage the best to remain with us?

First, it was important for us to share that we were not alone in our challenges. We also needed to show some signs of hope. We made sure everyone read our U.S. partner IDG's newsletters that featured case studies and gave them a view of where the publishing world was going. We went to conferences and even though money was tight, we took key salespeople and staff so they had an opportunity to talk to others around the world in our industry.

When IDG would put together its international conference in Boston for worldwide senior internal management and partners, we would take as many as 10 to 12 people. It got everyone on the same page and gave them the idea that we were indeed doing the right things. In some cases, we would discover that we were among the leaders in the world.

Our analytics staff was one of those places. We had a young man, Arnab Tagore, who did our first analytics on the websites. He did a beautiful job. We started working in Google Analytics very early and from a B2B perspective we were way ahead of most publishers at the time.

Ironically, however, as good as we were with analysis, we were struggling with execution. We had data, but we couldn't agree on what it meant. Even if we did agree on a direction, could we execute on it? We needed new leadership in several areas, but technology was first and foremost. If we did not solve our technical issues, nothing else was possible.

That's when Jim Love joined us. He was a consultant who came in to do some advisory on our CRM. Jim had experience as an executive and as a consultant with Ernst & Young and later DMR where he'd run a worldwide consulting practice. As luck has it, Jim had decided he'd had enough of corporate life and wanted to go back to hands-on consulting, so he'd started his own company.

Jim began to attend management meetings but was not a formal member of the management team. It was Brad McBride, our most senior salesperson who insisted that Jim was the most strategic thinker he'd seen from all the consultants we'd used.

Brad himself was invaluable in those early days. He was forced to continually reinvent our sales and offerings. As digital ad revenue shrunk, we focused more and more on lead generation to the point where in our later years publishing was a minor portion of our revenue with events, lead generation and later, digital content creation being the new core of our business. If we hadn't made those shifts and done them as quickly as we did, we would never have survived.

Change or die—while it's dramatic, it also sounds so simple and logical when you say it or see it written in a business book or PowerPoint presentation. When directions are not certain, and you are betting with the returns of the shareholders and the future of the staff, it's not that simple. Once you decide, you must be relentless about execution. Brad brought that determined relentless focus to our sales. We needed it throughout the organization.

Traditionally, the world of turnarounds of any sort is not forgiving. The world of digital transformation is even less so.

Taking stock

Here's the summary of where we were when we started our transformation.

We had shrunk enormously. One whole side of the office was almost empty, except for the writers in their cubicles. Somehow this added space enhanced the divisions in the organization. The writers were on one side, sales and administration far away on the other. On both sides those that remained fought for the status of the outside offices. Both sides of the floor were deathly quiet. The signs of business problems were obvious. It didn't take a rocket scientist to see it.

In terms of technology, there were a multitude of issues. The CRM system which was being developed to automate both Sales and Audience Relations, was still having problems. Beyond the functionality problems, there were real performance issues. The system was months and months behind and looked like it would never be finished. We had a bright young programmer working hard and developing new features but with little real direction. While he did the best that he could to fill the gaps in requirements, with the resultant constant reworking, the system was simply not advancing.

The problems were not only technical. The system at the meta level had been over-designed. It tried to automate everything, yet without a clear detailed logic on how things would actually work. Without clear direction, impossible since the processes of the organization were complex and in flux, the code had to somehow anticipate every possible option.

Someone had a fantastic imagination and vision but a total lack of understanding about the realities of development. Without tackling the issues in the underlying processes, the idea was to automate everything and every possible option—a strategy that almost never works and always underperforms.

Even with those great ideas, the details of the system were being designed in a vacuum. The business and IT divide meant that no one was participating actively. The salespeople didn't believe in the new system, the operations staff were too busy and even when they met, the resultant specifications merely asked IT to automate every possible variation, real or imagined, the technology equivalent of asking us to boil the ocean.

We did finally manage to get the sales CRM stabilized. That came at an expense. We had to first admit that much of what we'd done was useless and would never see the light of day. We ripped out the confusing and over-designed code and simplified the system. As a result of not throwing good money after bad, we got something up and running. Was it everything that was wanted? No. Not even close. But it ran. We began to make plans to complete some additional functions once we got the system into operation but first, we hired an analyst to work on understanding and perhaps even changing some of the business processes. Arlo Murphy, the analyst we hired, had advanced degrees in both IT and philosophy. In the constant uncertainty we faced, we joked that we were never quite sure which was the most valuable.

As we dug deeper, we found that CRM was the least of the worries. The content management system was in even worse shape—a half-finished disaster. While the basic functions had errors and issues, there were several futuristic projects attached to the system which were incomplete or not working at all. A 'semantic engine' was supposed to do text analysis and somehow use that information to help generate content suggestions. It was a clever concept, but it wasn't working and frankly, even if it ever did, there was no-one who understood how we would actually use it.

We ran our own office and mail systems including an exchange server, not uncommon for that time, but even our basic systems were problematic. It looked like (and later we found it was) someone's first attempt at implementing an email system by reading a how-to manual. Of course, as luck would have it, that person had left, but the structural issues remained.

Again, our one bright spot was the Google Analytics and SEO team. They were doing some interesting and even leading-edge work. But even that was hampered not only by the technology but also by the culture. They would produce reports, but few of these would be well used.

Most of the systems were hosted off-site, split between a facility in Toronto and another in the U.S. Both had something in common. They were very expensive and rigid. Every decision you made locked you into a multiple year contract for even minor services. When we needed more RAM on a server, we literally had to sign a multi-year rider to our agreement. There was little help or advice for us. The menu was there, selecting was our responsibility.

After a major server crash our Toronto hosting company blamed us for not having ordered the right backups. Someone from our organization had assumed that the snapshots our provider took would function as a backup. In some cases, they could—unless of course you experienced a total loss of the production image and attempted to rebuild on a new server. Which, of course, is what actually happened.

The hosting company admitted that the technical meltdown was their fault. But we were supposed to have backups. That is where we came to an understanding of what 'shared responsibility' was long before the term became popular. It meant, to us at least, that we were the only ones truly responsible for our data and security. It was a lesson we never forgot.

Culture wars

Despite the number of very talented people who were trying to do good things, IT was a mess, and not just from a technical standpoint. In fact, technology may have been the least of our issues. The politics, arguments and conflicts were constant. That there was any semblance of morale at all was probably the result of a young man who would later emerge as a leader of the IT Group – Matheepan Panchalingam (Matt Pancha for short).

Matt was a transplanted Texan who had a knack for ignoring the conflicts and keeping the team out of the fray. That talent would prove essential and he would later play a key role in the transformation.

The IT World Canada culture was toxic. Political intrigue abounded and conflicts were common. Although Fawn had been made president, it was by no means certain that she had the mandate to 'clean house.' Some of the people, including a sales VP had been hired by the owner and were actively working to unseat Fawn as president.

One of the ways that this VP was hoping to advance was through what he thought was his knowledge of IT. He refused to help and was abusive in ways that would not be accepted in any company today. In the IT World culture, however, he was just another tough 'hard hitting' executive and remnant of a past 'macho' culture run wild.

We had a lot to fix, little support and next to no money to do it. We knew it was bad. As we took stock, we felt that we were only beginning to realize was just how bad it was. Our feeling was, however, that unless you do an honest assessment and truly identify the issues, nothing will change. We pushed on.

Against the odds

There was a lot to do. We had little financial runway left. The odds were stacked against us. We did our assessment and we worked to fix what we could. We enlisted who we could, and we started to build a team. Our CIO, Jim Love ran interference while our new second in command patiently worked through our technical issues. Those who tried to pursue the old 'IT bashing' strategy found that Jim's experience as a consultant made him a very difficult adversary.

At the same time, the owner, Michael Atkins, announced that he was looking to put the company into receivership. This vaulted us into another crisis, one that we could not share with the larger team. While Michael mused, our burning question was, should we stop our transformation that had just begun?

We had another option. We could offer to buy the company. If we did, we had to tackle this and win. Our only remaining option was to get out quickly.

Logically, getting out might have been a good strategy. Both of us had options. But in the end, we faced a dilemma. We both wanted the company to survive. It was a Canadian icon. It filled a real role in the IT ecosystem. To see it wiped out was not acceptable.

As we sat in the office and wondered if we indeed could turn the company around, we had one more reason to proceed. Despite the number of people we had lost, there was a loyal, dedicated and talented team of people who worked very hard to be the best at what they did.

We decided that Fawn would take a proposal to Michael Atkins who had told her that he was seeking a receiver and possible bankruptcy. The two of us would offer to buy the company and bring it back from the brink. Our proposal to Michael was that we would add a minor amount of capital and that he would loan the business some additional funds. In return, we would agree to pay him back the money he had loaned the business over the years. Michael accepted the offer and fortunately, the other minority shareholder, IDG, also placed support behind our buy-in.

We still weren't thinking about anything as grand as a transformation at the time. We did know that we needed to act more like a start-up. We had to pivot and change direction.

We were determined to succeed. We knew that it wouldn't be easy. We were, however, determined to try.

The Dot-Customer

"People think that digital transformation is about technology. It's not. It's about the customer experience. Note that I didn't say customer satisfaction. I said customer experience. Customer experience is not about scores or surveys. It's about how customers feel when they deal with you. In one research paper we saw, 75% of customers who changed suppliers reported being 'satisfied' with their current provider. Satisfied is not enough."

- Jim Love, CIO, IT World Canada

Our journey of digital transformation has only served to reinforce our view that there is a new demand for an authentic customer experience and that the real secret of digital transformation lies in relentlessly driving to continually fulfil that demand. Technology unlocked the door, creating the conditions that empowered the customer. A purchaser now could move to another supplier with a click of their mouse. They were finally in charge. Once empowered, customers were free to express a real and visceral pent-up anger and frustration. They did.

Some blame the relative anonymity and lack of inhibition inherent in digital communication. Others point to the new ability to strike back when they felt they'd been wronged. It turns out they were both right. The Internet allowed the customer the power not only to find a new supplier but also to punish the prior offender by naming and shaming, first in websites and then on the newly emerging social media platforms. Whatever the reasons, the new customer was more knowledgeable, empowered and mad as hell.

The truth was that the anger and frustration that drove the great shift in customer attitudes had been developing over a long time. It was captured as far back as the 1976 hit movie *Network* written by Paddy Chayefsky. The movie featured a news anchor who starts a revolution. first getting noticed by threatening his own suicide and then leveraging that attention to get viewers to shout, "we're mad as hell, and we aren't going to take it anymore."

But consumer resentment goes even further back. In the 1960's baby boomers rebelled against the 'establishment.' Our love/hate relationship allowed us to simultaneously embrace and despise television, radio and commercial media. We loved the content, but at the same time knew we were being manipulated and resented it. That resentment grew as our standard of living and our newly acquired kids and mortgages forced many of us to become what we never thought we would—part of a middle-class establishment.

Without the large demonstrations of the 1960's our discontent was no longer dominant in the global media. We instead became the target of commercial forces via the one-way mechanism of commercial broadcast. We called it the 'idiot box' but we spent more and more time in front of it. We were now the obedient subjects of the consumer society and we resented it. But what could we do about it?

When, near the end of the century, multiple forces converged to create a two-way global network, it would change the power dynamic in ways that no Madison Avenue executive would ever have thought possible. We witnessed the birth of the 'dot-customer.'

The hallmark year was 1999, eight years after Tim Berners-Lee's creation of the World Wide Web became publicly available. It was an exciting and memorable year in the early digital age, a year where legacy and future states converged. It was a year full of hope and fear.

Fear came in the form of millennial anxiety. We faced the nightmare vision of a potential computer meltdown in a world which was increasingly dependent on its digital computer systems. Teams around the globe worked feverishly to avoid the potential Y2K disaster.

The fear was that computer systems would suddenly stop at the stroke of midnight on December 31, 1999. The two-digit fields that stored the date in many mainframe computers wouldn't be able to cope with the new century. What would happen to these systems that ran our banking, our stock exchanges, our airports, our power generation and distribution? Nobody really knew.

To some Y2K was an imminent disaster. To some it was overblown, over-hyped or simply a hoax. The only thing everyone did agree on was just how dependent we had become on networked computer systems.

Hope was also abundant in that magical year. The Internet, although it had taken decades to emerge, had been in the mainstream public for a scant five or six years. The slow networks and telephone modems made it mostly a novelty for many. Yet despite its limitations, in the year running up to the end of the century, we experienced a burst of millennial optimism and the beginnings of the dot-com bubble. Nothing was impossible. A bright new future was on the way in a new democratized world where the consumer was king.

Almost lost in all of this was a book launch of a new kind, one that fully exploited the power of the Internet. The *Cluetrain Manifesto* launched, fittingly, not with the usual media interviews, book tours or signings but on the Internet itself. Beginning with the phrase, "People of earth," it went on to dictate its new ninety-five theses, channeling Martin Luther's famous revolt against the Catholic Church that launched the Protestant Reformation. Rather than being nailed to a cathedral door, however, this manifesto was presented in the new public square—the World Wide Web.

The manifesto embraced the two-way nature of this new medium. It asked that readers sign their name, symbolically co-creating the manifesto and establishing joint authorship with the reader. It announced this two-way revolution as a 'new global conversation' and predicted a new era of communication we now know as social media. It foretold a revolution in which the customer could use the freedom of the Internet to stand up to even large corporations. It resonated with customers who had grown tired, angry, and frustrated with the way they were being treated and who feared a similar fate with the growing commercialization of the Internet. It announced:

"We are not seats or eyeballs or end users or consumers, we are human beings - and our reach exceeds your grasp – deal with it."

If Y2K realization tapped into our fear of how dependent we had become on our network of computer systems, the *Cluetrain Manifesto* fed our desire for the liberation that these same networks could bring to our lives. The Internet had initially been designed to communicate, as a means of free expression. In its early days, it was an anarchistic conversation with few rules and accessible to anyone. As it grew, however, it became more and more dominated by commercial forces.

The .org and .net domains gave way to an explosion of .com domains. The so-called dot-com bubble was growing. Companies with little more than a business plan were raising funds and selling at multiples that defied all investment logic. Especially among the pioneers and early adopters, there was a growing resentment of the commercialism of the Internet and the potential domination by the twin devils of Wall Street and Madison Avenue.

Then the other shoe dropped. The world held its breath on December 31, 1999 as the new year ticked into being. And nothing happened. Our fears, as it turns out, were groundless. The disaster never occurred. We may have dodged the bullet with the final rushed preparation. Or, as many felt, we had once again been duped. We were victims of an over-hyped non-event promoted by those who sought to control our new world and its technological infrastructures as they had with the old world. We suffered not catastrophe, but only embarrassment, as those who had bought generators and supplies for the apocalypse tried sheepishly to return them. Curiously, the lack of any impact seemed to increase the feeling of resentment of being once again manipulated by the one-way media.

A scant few years later we did experience a digital melt-down as the dot-com bubble burst and stock prices plunged. Companies that were worth millions were suddenly worthless. Those who invested lost terribly. For the majority of those hurt we shed no tears as a new cynicism and distrust of the commercial forces continued to grow. Despite these events, or perhaps because of them, over the next decade, the Internet would continue to change us all.

The emergence of e-commerce changed the way we purchased and shopped. The emergence of social media was about to also change the way we interacted, not only with each other but with corporations. As predicted in the *Manifesto*, the customer had found a voice and was empowered, impatient and outspoken in a way that was never before possible.

Interestingly, Doc Searls, one of the authors of the *Cluetrain Manifesto* later told us that reaction to the book was a huge surprise. It was written tongue in cheek, not as a joke but without the authors taking themselves too seriously. Yet, somehow, to their surprise, it tapped into a deep and powerful force of resentment and anger. That force, as the digital revolution proceeded, was profoundly changing customers and their behaviour. The result would shake the foundations of our markets, our commerce and our lives.

There was indeed a wave of change coming. First to feel the impact were those in publishing—books, music, periodicals and even the encyclopedia. Initially the effect of the Internet was positive. In the burst of optimism more websites appeared, and many predicted the need for an explosive growth in the production of content.

Content at that time was primarily the form of text but audio and video were developing as faster network and new digital tools became generally available. A new frontier was beckoning. The emergence of online advertising brought with it the promise of a new economic model. Entertainment was free, with the promise that it would be paid for by the necessary evil of advertising. It was similar to the framework we had lived with and accepted with radio and later, television.

But even in those heady times, the roots of future disruption were beginning to spread widely. There would be more and more content, but it didn't have to be supplied by what we classically thought of as publishers. In fact, publishers may have had an advantage initially, but it proved to be a temporary one. They had the skills, the writers, the graphic artists and they were eager to transfer these into this new world, a world which they saw as an addition to their print revenues. They didn't see the gifted amateur as competition, nor did anyone else.

That, it turns out, was a huge mistake. The Internet had been born from a frustration with broadcast, where we blindly sat and watched the one-way messages communicated to us by radio, television and even movies. The first public Internet was not very sophisticated to the user. A successor to the earlier bulletin boards, it existed primarily on something called telnet. By typing in 'nn' at the prompt, thousands of text chats from around the world— irreverent, blunt, sometimes downright pornographic and always wild—flooded in.

Much of it would make today's Reddit seem tame in comparison. We were no longer captives of one-way communication. Content creation and sharing was no longer the prerogative of the professional or corporate publisher.

Content spread in ways that no-one could have envisioned. The Internet provided a free means to share digital content of all types. Music, movies, software and even books that could be rendered in digital form were identical to their original. Piracy was rampant. Why pay for what you could get for free?

As the impact of piracy was hitting all forms of publishing, a second perhaps even more threatening underground movement had begun. Community created content had passed from the excesses of text in telnet to something with an emerging sophistication. Moreover, content was no longer just text.

An open source marketplace was emerging. Sophisticated software was being created by a community and distributed for free. Linux, the operating system that would dominate the infrastructure of the Internet, was a free download. Apache web servers were free. Even applications like Customer Relationship Management systems which cost tens of thousands of dollars could now be had for free, as software like the community creation SugarCRM went on to capture millions of downloads.

Musicians and video producers followed suit. They were bypassing standard publishers and going straight to the Internet with free downloads of increasingly sophisticated works. Books and other forms of content were being created and distributed by talented amateurs and even professionals, but with no cost to the reader. With the advent of licenses like the Creative Commons and others, the whole idea of paid content was being questioned, be it software, music, video or text.

As Dan Pink says in his famous TED Talk video "The Puzzle of Motivation" no sober economist in the right mind would have ever predicted that an upstart encyclopedia, written by volunteers would demolish not just the century old encyclopedia but would also defeat the well-funded and aggressively developed digital encyclopedia that Microsoft was launching at the same time. But Wikipedia did just that. The warning signs were there.

A new economic model was emerging to fit this new digital world and it threatened many of the established players.

Unfortunately, few print publishers saw it, including us— to our mutual peril.

Print publications were starting to make their content available on the web without the expectation of huge amounts of advertising revenue. Some did it primarily to remain relevant or as an advertisement for their highly produced print versions. These legacy publishers were about to get hit with a double whammy. They didn't have an effective way to monetize their digital content, at the same time as more and more consumers were finding their content online and questioning why they would bother paying for print subscriptions.

While print or hybrid publishers paid their writers, there was a new community, inspired by the open source movement which was providing free content. One new major competitor, the Huffington Post, took a page out of the Wikipedia playbook and emerged as a mainstream media competitor with a volunteer blogger network providing a great deal of their content. The mainstream media seemed oblivious to this new threat.

There is an old proverb that says, "whom the gods will destroy, they will first make mad." We have updated that to a modern version which says, "whom the gods will destroy they will first make rich." It illustrates our observation that the time just before digital disruption is often a period of high growth and profits.

It was certainly the case with BlackBerry. On the early days of the iPhone we asked a senior BlackBerry executive why they did not appear concerned, not about the phone itself but the huge number of applications that were being developed for the iPhone and sold for next to nothing or given away for free. His answer? "We sold more phones last quarter than in our history. This quarter, we are on track to break that record."

This was the world we lived in. In those heady days when print and online co-existed we saw the limitless growth in content consumption. We were part of that early development with new websites and a new frontier for technology journalism. But like so many others we missed the signs of just how big an impact and how far reaching the changes would be.

IT World Canada

IT World Canada was riding high in these early days, at least on the B2B side. In many ways, our model for B2B publishing seemed to be a perfect fit with the new online world. While we had a subscriber audience, we were not looking for paid subscriptions, so the model of the emerging free publications was not foreign to us. After we abandoned consumer publications, we were no longer in the group of publishers dependent upon subscription revenue. Our B2B audience received the publications for free with all costs paid by advertisers.

In our case, we had another positive characteristic in our existing model. Subscription was free, if your qualifications were relevant to the advertisers. This ensured that 100% of our audience was exactly what advertisers would pay to reach.

We had a clear advantage in terms of our sales. In the classic world of marketing that existed at that time, agencies controlled the advertising spend of most large companies. For us, selling was a relatively straightforward process. You built a qualified subscription audience and kept good relations with the advertising agencies. Revenue and profit would follow. That formula had fueled our growth for decades.

In our world, a premium was paid to those who had the best or biggest audience share and brand recognition. To get to the number one spot, IT World Canada made some key moves which would be very consistent with the classic Michael Porter model we discussed in the first section of this book.

The company had bought its biggest competitor, the previous number one publisher in the B2B tech space. From that acquisition IT World Canada instantly took over the number one spot. In the process, it also acquired new publications that expanded to include the line of business-oriented *IT Business;* a new but related audience of the many hardware, software and service providers called *Computer Dealer News* (now *Channel Daily News*), and the only North American IT French publication in print and online, *Direction Informatique,* for the Quebec market.

Earlier, IT World Canada had formed a partnership with international publisher IDG Group. IDG became a minority shareholder with a promise not to compete in Canada.

With IT World Canada's competitors out of the picture by purchase or partnership, the company was extremely well positioned in terms of brands and subscriptions. As the number one player in the market, our role was not *selling* to the agencies. We were *educating* them on the industry that we dominated. That's control. Under the classic Porter model, IT World Canada had done everything right.

We created programs like our 'agency days.' At that time, companies were spending a lot of money in print. Our goal was to teach the agencies how to direct that spending. We covered topics like what the IT end-user business was, why CIOs are so important, right down to what the difference was between a network analyst and a programmer. Our role was less sales and more facilitation and education. We prepared the agency so they could appear knowledgeable in their conversations with the end customer.

While the agencies were a main conduit for orders, we also retained a close relationship to big technology firms. We wrote about them. We interviewed them. We did special events with them. Our reputation and the international brands we took from our partner IDG made IT World Canada a very influential player.

Even while we made our content available on the websites, initially at least, our print did not suffer. Our CIO magazine was a great example. It captured the emerging new leadership of the IT function. If you ask any CIO about our magazine at the time, they will tell you what is was like to get your picture on that glossy cover in a magazine with high production values. It was not the same as having a picture on a website.

The emphasis was on the print subscription audience remaining intact and growing. Whether they read our content on the website or in print didn't matter. Our job was to simply ensure a print copy was received. Accordingly, the readership audits were at our own expense. They didn't have to read the publication thoroughly or even at all for it to count as circulation. However, you did need to prove the publications were accepted at delivery.

In fact, for print, there was no way to prove if anyone read anything. They could have skipped parts, simply put it on the table and replaced it when the next one arrived by mail. No matter. It counted. In fact, each subscription also had what was then termed a "pass along" rate. Each copy was assumed to have an actual 2.3 qualified readers as a 'pass along,' based upon extensive third-party studies.

Unknown to us, this was changing. As Internet publications became more and more the norm the content was now on the sites for everyone to read without subscription. In an Internet world, readers no longer had to qualify for subscriptions to read articles.

If they couldn't get it from you, the same information was a click away somewhere else.

Over time this had an enormous impact. We lost the status element of the publications. Having one of these publications on display in your office showed you had position and authority. You needed that to qualify for a subscription. It may sound strange or even petty, but the pre-Internet IT department was a very clear hierarchy where status and rank mattered, just like the business areas that IT served.

Your work area was directly related to your status. Workers had desks or cubicles. Supervisors and managers had bigger cubicles with room for a table in addition to their desk. Directors had a larger area and table, usually an office. VP's and that new creature—the CIO—would have a much larger office sometimes with a coffee table. Publications were not just reading, they were part decoration, and illustrations of your status. The electronic version made no such distinction and conveyed no status.

In response, IT World Canada and a lot of other publications attempted to replicate the subscription model by building a subscription form and an online audience management capability—what later came to be called in the industry as 'gating.' Gating was a total failure. No one cared.

Even in the early days, there were lots of sources of information that didn't require you to subscribe. Subscriptions went down to a trickle. The status factor of print publications was lost. Even if it was possible to gate publications and have subscriber-only content, the new online revenue models came not from subscriptions, but from the number of page views. Gating reduced the volume. Forcing anyone, even unqualified subscribers (or those who just didn't wish to qualify) to click elsewhere was counterproductive.

To add insult to injury, our experiment with gating was doubly doomed. Our legacy CMS was not easy to customize. Forcing everyone to log-in was not workable. Doing anything that would encourage a subscriber to register was impossible within the limitations of the system. As well, the complex questions we needed to ask to register someone new, while relatively easy on a printed form, were an awful experience in the drop-down world of web forms.

Within our Audience Services department we were busily trying to manage this new audience with the same tools and processes that we had used for our paper-based subscriptions. The impact of the failure of gating was yet to be felt but the costs and complexity of running print and digital side by side was stretching resources and putting increased demands on systems. Trying to do the right thing, without a new system to address the issues of digital publishing, our Audience Services processes became a kludge of old database programs and spreadsheets.

One saving grace was that under the leadership of our prior president, Andy White, we had bought a very sophisticated European enterprise email program called Messagent (now Selligent). With it, we had developed a huge list of email newsletters. That lucky break would prove to be one of the keys to our survival. Email newsletters, unlike website content, required a subscription with an accurate return address. We could still identify and classify our readership despite the anonymity of the websites and the inaccuracy of our print subscriber data.

Over the next decade publishers would work hard to win positions with the emerging search engines to increase their number of page views. In a world of a 'click away' the reader could exit to a competing site in Canada or the U.S. so being top of the search results was essential. But an email subscriber received regular content delivery without the publisher worrying about winning each search argument and as a bonus, without the cost of postage.

In this new world, analytics was everything. New programs and algorithms were emerging from the search engines that could tell you exactly which articles were searched, which were read and even how long they spent on each article or of increasing importance, how many ads were served to the reader. At the same time, Google was beginning to gather data and understand the behaviour of our audience, something that had once been our trade secret, shared with agencies and others in return for highly profitable advertising.

When content was delivered by email, we could tell that someone actually opened the email. There was no pass along factor, and we had yet to move to the actual sharing statistics from social media. But however minimal, we had some information that remained our proprietary data. Still, we could not ignore the search engines.

Email was a big asset, but where you appeared in the search engines and how many clicks came to your web pages were also very important. Unlike print, with its assumed 2.3 readers per copy delivered, you now earned every view, every click or you earned nothing.

The old strategy that had seemed so right under the guidance of Porter's model began to falter. Our brand names we had acquired, our number one position, all these costly things that were so powerful in the print world were lost in the Internet world. Search engines had negated even our geographic protection. Even our brand was diminishing. It mattered only if you were on the first page of a search. Without that, brand was irrelevant.

Even where brand factored into the readers' decisions, the Internet had turned our prior successful strategies against us. All IT World Canada's publication brands had identical names in the U.S. *CIO*, *Network World*, *ComputerWorld* and more existed in both countries. In print, this was a godsend. We had our local news and could also use the large cache of content generated by IDG's global brands.

Suddenly, our partner and shareholder IDG was beginning to look more and more like a competitor. Our agreement that granted their stake in the company had given us exclusive rights to the Canadian territory (and still does). But Internet readers might not differentiate between CIO as a Canadian site and CIO as a U.S. site.

In the days when size mattered more than anything and there was no geographic bias in the algorithms, the U.S. IDG site with a similar name also had an advantage in terms of winning the search argument. Their audience was ten times the size of ours. Our SEO geniuses headed by consultant David Jonah and brilliant young staffer Arnab Tagore led a continual struggle to win Canadian search results from everyone, including our U.S. partner.

The partnership with IDG had led us to change our name and flagship site to IT World Canada. Now we had a competitive site with the same name as our Canadian site that was a click away. Traffic that went to the U.S. sites earned us nothing.

Not only had we lost all advantage from our brands, but to make matters worse we risked losing control of our brand identity. The U.S. flagship site, which bore the similar name ITWorld.com, began as a low-quality site that was little more than a search engine farm. It focused on volume with apparent little regard for the quality of its content.

On the other hand, quality was essential to us. Our niche audience's perception mattered in this new world where the customer—the reader—was in total control. Choices of what to read were indeed only a click away. As search engines increasingly drove access, our number one status in print diminished in importance. Moreover, a significant amount of our revenue came from our status in the industry, not just with the agencies but also with corporations and governments where our events earned us a huge and growing portion of our revenue. Any perception of diminished quality could have a real impact on our ability to attract a status conscious audience or advertiser.

In search of that reader experience, like other large publishers, we invested heavily in our content management systems (CMS). But new niche competitors were emerging on free web servers that could serve specific portions of the audience. Where publications like *Computerworld* or *Network World* could serve a wide audience in print, new micro-targeted sites could drill down to even a specific programming language or a single network product.

What might have seemed to be the last remaining advantage—our pool of journalists—was losing its power as a barrier to entry. A small competitor could open with one writer skilled on a specific topic. Increasingly, these writers need not even be paid.

The new amateur journalist—the blogger—was emerging. As individuals or in emerging sites like the Huffington Post the competition of the blogger was beginning to have an impact on us and anyone else where paid journalism was the base of their content.

All these options were served to an audience to whom brand loyalty was no longer a ticket to readership. Even those who loved our brands were reading a range of other publications. We were feeling the initial impact of digital disruption.

Our legacy assets and all the things that had made IT World Canada a success in the market were either diminishing in importance, had less value, or in some cases were actively competing against us. Customer loyalty was no longer a function of brand or market position. You won each customer, article by article, page view by page view. Competition came from all sides.

The rules of customer interaction were being re-written. A new era was beginning.

Outrun the Bear

"We should emphasize that we didn't know at the time we were embarking anything as grandiose as a 'digital transformation' strategy. We thought we were doing something bold - what our CIO Jim Love called a 'burn the boats strategy.'"
— *Fawn Annan*

The Economics of Digital Transformation

We knew we were stopping print and keeping our digital properties. We also knew that we had a 'revenue hole' that we had to fill. That was how we saw our challenge. We were about to learn that these were the easiest problems to deal with as we received a hard lesson in digital economics and the new rules of digital competition.

It's very easy to look back on organizations that were blindsided and that have not survived a market shift and say, "That's why it happened. It's obvious." It's quite another thing to live through it in real time. When we were going through this, we were hearing dire predictions, and from time to time seeing examples of what was happening. But for most of our working days, which were long and exhausting, we were focused on the day to day problems.

The brutal reality is that we were still dominated by the immediate issues of plummeting revenue and its impact on our very survival. Reflection was not a luxury we could afford. Or to put it in the vernacular, "it's hard to drain the swamp when you are up to your ass in alligators."

Even if we could find the energy or time and step back with some degree of objectivity during this major shift in our business what good would it do? It may suit an industry guru to admire the problem, but did they really have the solutions?

After Y2K, the dot-com bubble and a host of other would be disasters, would you believe every guru, every business book, every new trend, every headline? For a business owner, or anyone with real profit and loss responsibility, the answer is categorically, no. The risks are too great. It's not that business owners are incapable of understanding problems and evaluating their options. But having to do this when you think you can no longer trust your business education and your prior experience feels like jumping without a parachute.

Our problem was compounded by an investor who had spent years in the print business and who appeared to be feeling pressure from all sides. Everything that had worked in the past was no longer working. His other print media businesses, the ones that remained, would have been under the same threats. He had exited from his earlier weekly news ownership and only the flagship Northern Life and its extended properties remained.

Northern Life was local news in Sudbury. It was also, like all weeklies, the vehicle for a booming flyer business. In addition, it had other specialty print publications aimed at the north and northern industries. We, on the other hand, moving to a fully digital stance, were harder to understand. Our former owner was questioning us at a time when we had no guaranteed answers. He was also losing faith, not in us, but in the viability of the business.

No doubt his other business was also challenged. Weekly publications were feeling the same forces as daily newspapers with declining revenue and circulation, albeit at a slower rate, but just as real. In addition, other economic factors were also affecting them as they were all publications.

Retail, an industry that was under attack by e-commerce was struggling and the consolidations and closings were affecting the number of companies who wanted to advertise. Fewer customers meant fewer flyers, to all weeklies. Between that and the emergence of digital coupons, the drop in the once lucrative flyer business certainly created a huge revenue gap for many weeklies.

Outside of casual conversations we couldn't be certain, but if Northern Life were like every other publisher, it might be experiencing the same difficulties. The new Sudbury.com was certainly doing well, at least in terms of the awards it was winning. Whether successful or not, we knew firsthand that any print business is a struggle. We were just one more problem. Even after we took over majority ownership, Michael remained, but his heart was no longer in it. As financial pressures mounted, squabbles broke out between the former chair and the two new shareholders. These weren't personal in nature, they stemmed from the new economic reality that we confronted. They were, however, a painful distraction from the task at hand.

Our lesson in the new rules - outrunning the bear
There's an old joke about two people out in the woods who come across a fierce bear about to charge them. In response, one

of the two men bends down and fixes the laces on his track shoes. His frightened colleague says, "what are you doing? You can't outrun the bear." The other person continues to lace up his shoes and says with a grin, "I don't have to outrun the bear. I just have to outrun *you*."

The bear seems at first to be a fitting metaphor for the fundamental shift in the rules of economics and competitive behaviour that accompanies digital disruption. We were under attack. We could stick to the old ideas that competitive forces operated in the new world exactly as they had in the past. But our competitors refused to follow the rules. Apparently, they only had to outrun us.

But in this topsy-turvy world even the bear doesn't follow the rules. We would find out that the bear has a voracious appetite. Having devoured a weaker competitor, he does not stop. He still comes bounding after you. Finding solutions to try to address new competitors, even winning battles with them means little when the appetite is insatiable and the force is unstoppable. Today, you must outrun the bear, at the same time as the pace of change—the speed of the bear—accelerates.

The old rules and the old metaphors may have served us in earlier times, but the rules have changed, and the old metaphors have lost their relevance. We need new symbols to illustrate our new thinking. Jim Collins offers one. He uses the model of a flywheel to show how change accelerates and how we might understand its impact.

Collins' flywheel is based on the mechanical device that stores and regulates energy and motion. In the early stages, it takes a lot of energy to get a flywheel started, but after a time it builds up momentum. Once it reaches its peak energy, it becomes a nearly unstoppable force requiring only minor energy to maintain its power of forward movement, but tremendous power to stop or reverse it. Collins used this as an illustration of momentum in business. In the initial stages, the pace is slow. But there is a point where the force builds and when it does hit its stride it moves relentlessly forward.

That's where we were. The forces that had started so slowly—declining revenue, high costs, increasing competition—were gaining momentum. We had yet to see the real problems clearly, let alone find solutions to slow or stop the build-up of energy. We had to stop this flywheel before it overwhelmed us.

The problem we thought we were solving

Initially, like many businesses that encounter revenue challenges, we thought we were dealing with a cost issue. If revenue dropped, we did our best to bring our costs into line. We reduced staff, cut expenses and did everything we could to lower costs with our shrinking revenue, hoping to get some level of equilibrium while we recovered. With limited resources, these actions are essential, and it is unlikely that we would have survived without cost containment and reduction. Unfortunately, they were simply not enough and never would be.

There is a saying that "you can't cut your way to greatness." In the digital world, the dilemma is especially poignant. We had to find a revenue model that would focus on growth but equally allow us to get the margins necessary to do our business well. Despite that, if we didn't manage expenses and deal with the rapid revenue loss fast enough, we wouldn't live to fight another day. But in our hearts, we knew that we really had a revenue problem, not a cost problem.

But how could we find a new revenue model— and find it quickly? We realized that declining revenues were the result of commodification, a failure to prove our true value. We knew, as we state in our chapter on the dot-customer, that value can only have one expression as that which creates an outstanding customer experience. Everything else is just cost or procedure that customers don't want, are unwilling to pay for and may even resent.

We had to balance our cost reduction with the search for a new revenue model. With the speed at which revenue was dropping, both actions were going to need to be extreme. But the danger of radical cost surgery is you don't know when you are no longer cutting fat and when you are into the muscle and sinew needed to operate or in this case, rebuild a product offering. Are you cutting cost or value? The secret is you that need to proceed knowing you will make mistakes and inevitably cut into muscle and bone. The only thing you can do is as little damage as possible. What we had to avoid at all costs, was hitting an artery. But unless you clearly understand the difference between value and cost, you are operating with a blindfold on.

This is where another of Collins' models served us well. It is one of the few that not only endures, but seems tailor made for this new era. Collins' developed what he called a 'Hedgehog Strategy.' The name originates from a Greek proverb, "the fox knows many things, but the hedgehog knows one big thing." In other words, a great strategy is based on one simple idea, which is that 'one thing,' the true value in your organization and offerings. That value and the strategy to create it can be found in the answer to three questions.

- What are you passionate about?
- What can you beat the world at?
- What are the metrics that drive your economic engine?

The intersection of your passion and areas of your greatest ability establishes where you can create unique value. In a hyper-competitive market, it's essential that you find that point of convergence and leverage it to create a unique value proposition.

There is a frequent trap, one which is easy to fall into and it hit us as well. Often, when value is questioned, salespeople mistake value for including more in the same cost envelope and calling that 'value add.' While appearing to make progress, this only adds to cost and exacerbates the problems of profitability. It also becomes both a slippery slope and a vicious cycle as customers demand more and more for less and less. When this happened, we would win new accounts and projects, but we would still find ourselves facing losses despite the increase in revenue. Sales and operations morale plummeted as overworked staff rebelled at taking on extra work with less resources.

Companies that are successful settle for nothing less than an exceptional experience for the customer, but they do that in a way that is profitable. They don't simply add more for less, they focus on what truly adds value which is, by the only correct definition, what a customer will pay for given a choice.

Finding that simple and powerful value requires two elements which we are rarely focused on in business—passion and purpose. Customer experience is an emotional experience, an expression of the passion for a desired purpose as felt by the customer. We cannot tap into that unless we can find it in ourselves and our companies.

Many of us have been taught that there is a separation between ourselves as people and the objective rules that govern business. Even the phrase 'it's just business' reveals our attempt to keep that artificial division. That compartmentalized view may have been sustainable in the past, but in the world of digital transformation it is not in synch with the desire for authenticity and the need for highly motivated, committed and empathetic staff. Digitally enabled companies may have less employees, or a highly elastic workforce, but they all absolutely need a skilled, engaged and most importantly, a committed staff. A competitive customer experience is simply not possible without these essential components.

The digital world has perfect price competition, an informed and highly impatient customer and requires no less than a world class effort regardless of your size or resources. That, in turn, demands an unwavering commitment from all levels of the company. Without passion and belief, that level of commitment in a time of great uncertainty is simply not possible.

This emphasis on emotional response and intrinsic motivators like passion and purpose does not mean that we abandon science and logic. We must pay attention to science, but that is, as it turns out, not incompatible with the idea of passion and purpose as the new motivating factor. In a 2009 TED Talk, *The Puzzle of Motivation*, author Dan Pink makes the case that purpose is ignored because there is a "gap between what science knows and what business does."

Pink goes on to argue that the types of rewards and incentives that are often used in business are actually counterproductive. In a carefully structured argument, he shows that in multiple studies from conservative, free enterprise think-tanks ranging from the London School of Economics to the Federal Reserve in the United States the conclusive findings were that classic, economic based incentives hinder creative work and stifle innovation.

Pink is not claiming that you don't have to pay employees fairly. The lack of a fair wage is a disincentive. What he does claim, backed by strong research, is that if you motivate employees only with financial rewards—the proverbial carrot and stick—you will impair their ability to function at their creative peak. What does he prescribe? Pink claims in his 2009 book, *Drive* that there are three key factors. They are autonomy, mastery and—there's that word again—purpose. Pink and the research he cites show that to motivate, inspire and empower people you need to find your purpose as an organization and express that purpose clearly, authentically and continually.

Stating our purpose was simple. We exist to create engaging content that tells the stories of technology in business to our corporate audience. It is simple, clear and consistent with our history as publishers and community builders.

Later, in an attempt to define and develop that purpose we would have to grapple with what 'engaging content' truly is. To have value to our audience our content must help them in real and practical ways— make better decisions, enhance their careers or inform them about something they should not miss out on. Placed through this filter of real value, we started to question every aspect of the content we produced.

One might think that this would be an easy sell to our editors and writers. They idea of purpose and value to the reader should be welcomed with open arms. On a conceptual level, it was. When it got to the details, surprisingly, we had issues with those whose job it was to create content.

Our editors were trained as journalists. They reported the news objectively. As trained journalists, they felt they knew what was newsworthy and what was not. In the old print world, where we were primarily a one-way medium, this may have been sufficient. In the new hyper-competitive world, it was not.

We needed the journalists to develop a meaningful conversation with their audience. Their first response was that "we already do that." When pushed, they offered the usual idea. We had in the past done audience surveys. Why not do another? This in our opinion, missed the point and was not what we needed.

There is some value to surveys, but they are major undertakings and only provide information at a point in time. In a rapidly changing world this is not sufficient. We also had a suspicion that many surveys merely confirm the bias of the questioner. You only get answers to the questions you ask, and in many surveys, the answers only happen in the context of the options we allow. Even if we got past those reservations, we also could not see how we would get the depth of insight, the immediacy and continuous dialogue we needed to generate great, highly engaging content.

We wanted something different. We were looking at nothing short of an authentic, open ended, two-way conversation. We knew what we needed to do. The question was how? In a digital age, how does a company have real conversations with its customers?

Web-site analytics gave us a better understanding of what content was successful. We could see the numbers in Google Analytics including time spent on pages and different engagement metrics. This motivated our journalists. We even had a plastic pitchfork that was circulated to the person who achieved the highest page views that week.

Over time we started to question the validity of this approach. Was time spent really engagement? Plus, in the days of print, our audience was restricted to IT decision makers and influencers. We had specific filters to ensure that we had the right audience. In the new world of digital content, we could no longer guarantee who was reading our content. So, the question arose that even if we get lots of views, are we reaching the *right* audience?

We had some additional tools to use. Our email newsletters gave us some information. We could tell who got what and if it was opened. Still, we needed more feedback. We put pressure on our journalists to get out and talk to the audience. This again met with some unexpected resistance.

We discovered that as long as we kept 'knowing the customer' on an objective or high level, we were fine. We all agreed that instead of 'pushing' content to our readers that we needed to 'pull' readers to us and in the process, learn what they needed. It was wonderful as a theory. It was when we tried to put it into practice that it became difficult in practice. Resistance was articulated in different ways.

We were told that focusing on the audience we could monetize could interfere with the objectivity of the journalistic process. Or in less guarded moments we were asked why we were questioning their skills and competence. Wasn't the job of a journalist to bring their audience what they *should* know?

One of our editors left because of the push to write not what he thought best, but to pursue our specific audience needs. In another case, we let an editor go because of his refusal to engage with an audience. He spent a major part of an exclusive annual CIO conference sitting alone at a desk typing a story. When we pushed him to engage more, we were told his priority—his job—was to file a story. We parted ways after that and looked to find someone who would embrace our idea that we needed to understand and engage the audience on a new level.

We came to realize that despite agreeing we must embrace the 'two way' nature of content, proven with the growing importance of social media, our publishing was still being created in the old one way 'broadcast' model. Analytics were not being used to understand the audience but to justify what the editors believed was right. The 'pull' model of discovery of how to meet your targeted audience was met with resistance.

It would take an almost total shift in editorial staff to get to the point where we studied both the analytics and worked hard to get to know the audience. To lead this, we took a chance on a younger editor, Brian Jackson. Brian understood the power of analysis and although reserved by nature, he made a real attempt to truly understand our audience and to pass that on to our other writers. Even with this agreement, we continued to have many passionate debates as we worked towards a new understanding of publishing for our community.

We brought the same passion for value to our commercial content. We appointed our CIO, Jim Love as Chief Content Officer with a mandate to engage and help us to understand our IT audience. Fawn, with her marketing background, took on a similar role on two fronts. She was to engage the Chief Marketing Officer, a role that was growing in importance as marketing and other line of business functions increasingly participated in or even led technology decisions. She would also champion our push to reach a female audience, another under-served but important group. We pushed, sometimes with limited success but great determination, to define data driven personas for our key audience segments and to test and further develop these in person with groups and one on one engagements with our audience.

From a technology perspective, we were also at work to get meaningful targeted analytics derived from audience behaviour in order to help build these essential personas. Once again, our email newsletters provided us with a key. We could identify this audience and monitor parts of their online behaviour. This in turn enabled creation of digital personas built on behavioural models of our actual audience. What we developed remains our trade secret, but we at last had a means of better understanding our audience, their behaviour and what that meant about their perception of the value of our content.

Value is what a customer will pay for when given a choice

Our need to slash our costs as revenue dropped continued to present us with challenges. How could we do all of things that we needed to transform the organization and maintain an excellent customer and audience experience with continually declining resources?

To deal with this we turned to what we've termed 'white collar Lean'. Lean, for those unfamiliar with it, was in manufacturing, what had vaulted Toyota to the number one spot in the automotive world. Although it is often thought of a Japanese invention, with its cryptic terms that evoke images of martial arts, it was in fact invented by an American, W. Edwards Deming.

Deming tried to engineer processes and work activities focusing on value driven metrics. His definition of value was unique and inspired what came to be known as Lean Manufacturing or 'Lean' for short. In Lean, anything that does not generate value for the customer is waste. Value can only be defined by *'what the customer will pay for if given the choice.'*

That relentless focus on value as seen through the eyes of the customer forces you to look at every step of every process and question it. In practice this generates some tough challenges.

Lean requires us to change a lot of our habitual behaviour. It forces us to question everything we learned not just about operations but also about management. While intellectually we can accept that setup time is a waste, it's hard to avoid the interruptions that cause others to have to stop and restart a process, which then requires an additional setup cost. All too often 'value destroyers' stem from management dictums and behaviours. In our culture, it was common for management to interrupt and call someone into a meeting to address an immediate issue with little or no regard for what was interrupted. The behaviour spread widely, and we acquired what our CIO termed a 'culture of interruption.'

Another area that is easy to absorb intellectually but tough in practice is how Lean insists that multiple quality checks—the essential controls of the modern office—are waste. No customer would pay for you to do a job twice. They would insist, as Lean does, that you get it right the first time.

Nor would they pay for someone 'a level above you' to check your work. In Lean, any control that retroactively tries to find errors is waste. If you follow Lean to its logical outcomes much of what we think of as supervision or management falls directly into the definition of waste.

Our embrace of Lean would inevitably conflict with our hierarchical culture. As we will discuss in the chapter *Culture*, IT World Canada was hierarchical and highly structured. In HR, for example, we had everything one would associate with a much larger company including several levels of management for HR to deal with. We also had all the overhead and bureaucracy associated with those structures. Parting with the rituals, structures and learned behaviours of that culture would prove to be very difficult.

We struggled with the process and cultural changes, but in the end, necessity forced our hand. Still, we further struggled, as so many do, with the definition of waste in terms of supervision and often several levels of checking and approvals. How could we be sure that work is done, and done correctly if no one checks it? But Lean thinking forced us to consider how much time is used in these steps. The amount of time used in redundant checking and retroactive fixes, if you truly tabulate it, especially in repetitive processes, can be astonishing. We desperately needed to recoup the lost time. We could not afford the extra cost of wasted effort.

There is a story from when Toyota partnered with GM at a plant in North America. A U.S. auto worker proudly showed his Japanese counterpart their quality checking. The Japanese worker trained in Lean was puzzled by the rubber mallet at the station and asked what they used it for. The American told him that they used it to fix doors that were out of alignment and demonstrated what they did, pounding the doors until they closed properly. The Japanese worker was still visibly perplexed. The American asked him, "how do you deal with doors that don't fit properly?" The Japanese worker answered simply, "we make them fit properly when we install them."

The Toyota auto worker could not imagine allowing errors to creep into the process to be pounded out or fixed retroactively. They are trained to appreciate the real costs. That is why Japanese autoworkers were allowed to stop the assembly line to prevent a problem early rather than fix it later at greater expense and effort. The fact that no American auto worker would have done the same is why Toyota surpassed the big three automakers. This is not some unique feature of the Japanese culture, and that was proven when that shared GM plant moved from 'worst to first' achieving high levels of quality by fixing problems at their root cause and eliminating redundant 'quality control.'

We looked at duplication and redundancy and removed everything we could. It was very uncomfortable at first. As predicted in Lean, quality did not diminish, it actually improved. In fact, our refusal to check some things established clearly that our employees had to get it right the first time. There was no 'safety net.' Yet, there are always errors and with each one, we fought to not regress back to the old costly multi-level checking.

Over time, our focus on measurement started to win the day. While resistance remained, we realized we could no longer afford to have the rigid structure of the old paper based, 1970's style organization. We had to become a truly Lean organization focused on value for our audience and customers. In today's hyper-competitive world, nothing less will do. It took time, determination and could be a little nerve-wracking to implement, but it paid off. Our motto had become:

Value is only what a customer will pay for when given a choice.

Using customer value to guide kept us from making some early and perhaps unrecoverable strategic errors. Pursuit of customer value became our best guide through many different decisions.

As the publishing industry problems became far more pronounced, multiple companies developed solutions to make audience management technology more affordable. We were offered many database and analytics solutions, sold as tools essential to a publisher's survival in the new digital era. These promised to help us understand our audience and monetize that understanding. Built in analytics would help us create targeted content and advertising with at a price far lower than our current costs and offering immediate ROI.

Tempting as they were, we worried that if we simply hopped aboard someone else's solution, we took a lot of risks. If the provider was to stay on top of what was needed in the marketplace, they would have to analyze our data as well as that of every other company using their software. The results of that analysis and the possible solutions would likewise become their asset and would be shared among their customers, if not directly, at least in terms of any new functions or tools.

Every time we looked at these offerings, we asked how they affected our ability to generate unique value. How vulnerable would it make us? Would we lose our unique understanding of our data? Would it add to or reduce our ability to be the only source of that understanding for our niche audience? We did this for all suppliers but particularly when the offeree was also a publisher or in anyone who might sell the insights from the data they stewarded.

We also wondered what would happen if we were on a shared solution and wanted to leave? What if the services were not what we needed? These were relatively new offerings and would need continued development. What would we do if they didn't advance? What if they raised the price of the service in the future? We had suffered through a similar problem with a video solution that we had bought. It attracted us with a low price in the first years, but we found at the end of our contract as we came to renewal, the price increased exponentially. Having no way out, we agreed to pay the new fees, but only until we could find an alternative.

When the decision did not involve our 'crown jewels,' our reaction was different. We used shared or commercially available systems wherever we could although we still asked the key question, "how would we get out of a SaaS or cloud structure if it ceased to meet our needs?" We didn't want what industry guru Don Tapscott had once termed the 'Hotel California' syndrome, based on the old Eagles lyric that "you can check out anytime you like, but you can never leave." That was all too prevalent in the early cloud and we avoided it by asking the right question and insisting on standards and exit plans. But where the audience database or the analytics and insights from that database were concerned, we felt that all the solutions on the market were far too risky.

We could only grow in this hyper-competitive world if we could analyze, measure and establish the value of our audience to advertisers and sponsors. To establish that value, we had to leverage our knowledge and find unique ways to be valuable to our audience. We were already thinking more in terms of community and experience than simply audience. We were diving into analytics to try to understand what drove engagement. We were building the idea of personas to increase our understanding.

But our legacy systems were a serious impediment to us. Not only could we not get the data we needed, but they were on their last legs. The expense of maintaining them was killing us, but we didn't have the money to replace them. We had to find a better solution without selling the crown jewels or putting us into a long-term and risky commitment.

We took the open source database of an existing CRM and leveraged that as the home of our audience management system at least in the short run. We shopped diligently for some analytics tools to use on that database. With open standards we were able to select from a number of tools. Ultimately, we would use open source frameworks to create a unique audience database linked to our CMS.

Cost was an overwhelming issue with us, but even if we'd had more money to spend, insisting on open standards would have been the right choice. In a world of digital economics, you must never be locked in or controlled. Your customers are not. Neither should you be. Open *source* was excellent in terms of cost, but open *standards* were non-negotiable.

A second reality was facing us. Digital advertising continued to become more and more commoditized. Ad networks and auctions were emerging which drove prices to incredibly low levels. Questions were coming back from our salespeople. "Why should customers pay a premium price for our digital advertising when they could buy it at a fraction of a dollar on auction?"

We did try to become a digital ad broker in our own right. We had a lot of knowledge. Our partner IDG in the US was moving forward with this aggressively selling their residual inventory.

After several false starts we were forced to abandon the idea of participating in ad networks. We couldn't compete with the others in this emerging area and sales were disappointing. We didn't have the huge page inventories of our US partner. Our operation was too expensive to support on the revenues we could earn from simply turning our inventory over to an ad network, even if we could gain a modest premium which was unlikely given market forces.

Our failure was a fortunate accident, because it forced us to once again go back to a strategy based not on finding the lowest cost but in focusing on the maximum value to the customer.

We didn't see this as fortunate at the time. We saw it as a crisis. We were hurting financially, and digital advertising revenue was falling rapidly. We desperately needed some success. Others claimed to be making money by selling inventory on ad networks. Our only result from all this effort was to learn another painful lesson in digital economics.

It took us a few years to realize that we could never have won in the world of commodity digital auctions. We didn't have the size or the scale to succeed. Even if we did, the downward price spiral promoted by the auction of inventory in a commodity market made it ultimately not a business that we would want to be in. Having failed, we had no option but to focus on building a premium value offering and finding a way to stay out of the ad networks. This turned out to be the right choice.

Several years later we have worked out a partnership with another large publisher and have inherited the best of both worlds. We have access to their large distribution and network which is many times the size of our database. They, in turn, were only interested in us because they couldn't get this level of understanding of our niche audience anywhere else.

We could never have predicted this. But understanding and relentlessly following 'value as defined by our customers' has been the one constant that has held true for us. When all else has failed, focusing on understanding customer experience and generating unique value has served us well.

Play by the new rules.

We were learning that we could not succeed if we played by the old rules. We needed to learn and confront the new rules of digital competition. We had to change how we saw the world and how we behaved. Here are some of the things we were thinking as we looked to find and understand those new rules:

- in a world where there is almost zero capital investment to enter a market and where the cost of production and distribution approaches zero, everyone is a potential competitor.

- when hyper-competition takes over, price competition leads only to a downward spiral. You need to find ways to compete based on a unique value proposition focused on knowledge and delivery of a unique user experience. That is the hardest thing to replicate. You must guard that understanding and ability as your most precious corporate asset.

- the customer is in control and the only definition of value is what they will pay for given the choice. Their decisions are not always logical. They are based on how the customer feels about their experience of your offering.

In the digital world, we were facing competitive pressure from everyone. Starting a new tech news site was not difficult at all. We had paid millions just a few years back to acquire our competition and now new competitors were emerging everywhere. Amateurs and even professional writers were starting up their own blogs and sites. This in turn, introduced us to another discovery about digitally disrupted competition:

In a world of digital disruption, where the cost of entry, production and distribution approach zero or are very low—legacy organizations are highly vulnerable and the leaders in a sector may be the most vulnerable.

Legacy organizations have staff, equipment, investments and skills. These were once effective tools to defend their competitive position and barriers to entry in their market. Today, these were impediments to value and unnecessary costs.

We understood that we had to compete on value, but the rules of how to do that had changed. A model developed by two Harvard professors, Michael Treacy and Fred Wiersema in their seminal book the *Disciplines of Market Leaders*' had years earlier established that that to compete on value, you needed to excel at one primary dimension and needed only to match your customers on the two other dimensions. The three dimensions were cost and efficiency, product or service innovation and customer intimacy. This theory had achieved the status of 'general wisdom' and was even embedded into models such as the *Balanced Scorecard*, which grew from Kaplan and Norton's ground-breaking work from the 1990's.

In the digital age finding one dimension to excel and matching the other two no longer worked. Companies now need to excel at all three dimensions. Knowledgeable customers expected the lowest price, the highest quality and an exceptional experience. Fulfilling all three is the ultimate aim, but when push comes to shove, we avoid anything where we can't ultimately compete on customer value and experience. Without that, any offering becomes commodified and faces an almost inevitable downward spiral of revenue as hyper-competition takes effect.

Another challenge for a legacy company is that once you have a large enough number of customers, some basic statistical rules fall into play. Any company of a certain size, if it analyzes its customer base, and takes the full costs into account, will find that statistically they have relatively few customers that are very profitable. The majority of their customers are only marginally profitable and even losing money. To maintain size and scale legacy companies must defend their entire base even while knowing that not all customers are equally valuable. A digital competitor, however, needs only to steal a small portion of customers. If they are the most profitable, the competitor can do extreme damage by stealing as little as a few key customers and in some cases, only one.

The costs of a legacy organization are often inelastic, and do not move in lockstep with revenue. A disruption in revenue can kickstart a cycle of continuous price cutting which in is extremely damaging to profit margins.

If a new company enters a market with a structural cost advantage, a legacy company can no longer respond solely by strategic or matching price cuts using their wealth to outlast the new entry until they relent and raise their prices or retreat. If the new entrant's costs are structurally lower, elastic, or worse— both— *they* will outlast the legacy firm, who will waste valuable time and resources that should be spent on transforming their enterprise to endure inevitable future assaults.

In the new world, we were, albeit in a small market, a legacy market leader. While we didn't have the size of our global competition or even of other media companies, we still had huge vulnerability. New competitors didn't need to be burdened with our cost structure. Nor did they need to go after all our customers. Like most companies, the bulk of our profits came from a relatively small number of our customers. They only had to attack the vital few.

Who is your competitor? Everyone.

In the world of print after the acquisition of our major competitor and the deal with IDG, IT World Canada may have been lulled into the idea that we had no competitors of any significance. We'd done the right things under the old rules. We'd paid a lot and carried significant debt, but we'd received a lot in return besides simply the exit of a competitor. We got our line of business and channel publications as well as some first-class talent in that purchase. We'd struck a deal many years back with the U.S. firm who could have been a major competitor. In return for a minority stake in the company we had our own territory— Canada.

We had built some flagship events and a reputation which dominated the event landscape in Canada including the prestigious Lac Carling, which brought together governments which were a major part of the purchasing landscape. We'd extended that event dominance to new areas such as our channel events which dealt with all the players in that marketing ecosystem in Canada. Events now accounted for more than a third of our revenue.

Then came the storm. In the new digital world, new competitors arose from everywhere. Some were small start-ups. Some were independent writers with lifestyle businesses. Then came the new onrush of free bloggers trying to make their name, get exposure and have their own portion of the readership.

More and more competitors attacked using variants on these new models. The Huffington Post used volunteer writers to fill their columns, some of which were about technology. Others discovered that they didn't have to create content on the web, they could simply curate the best that was out there. Both strategies offered scale and had no cost of content creation.

Even our clients became competitors. We had for years been one of the only ways that technology companies would advertise in a B2B market. Our clients had their own websites which no longer held only product and marketing materials. They were starting to produce some relevant and engaging content.

Our clients were starting to look more and more like publishers. With the advent of content marketing, where you offer an interesting piece of content for download, they were starting to develop and publish content that looked more and more like what we would develop. They were also hiring writers to produce their own blog content to attract an audience. We knew this was a serious threat when our Editor-in-Chief ended up at one of our larger clients building their content publishing.

Times were changing as associations and organizations we had worked with in the past were building their own web content portals. They were trying to establish their value with their members and stakeholders by creating and publishing content.

Simultaneously, we were also fighting an encroachment from other publishers who were adding or enhancing their technology offerings. Fighting the onslaught of declining revenues and a need for more page views to feed their advertising revenue, they developed new technology sections.

Everyone, it seemed, wanted to be like us.

If this weren't enough, with revenues dropping in publishing, American companies were selling a North American audience strategy. Even our own U.S. shareholder had a large amount of organically generated Canadian traffic on their sites. We protested, and even had real time examples, but making the case they had violated their agreement was difficult. We were once protected by geographic location, but on the Internet the reach of advertising campaigns became even more challenging and borders were being erased.

Another wave of competition came from social media players like Facebook and Linked In. Google, already providing our competitors with a way to achieve distribution via search was also moving into content curation. As these large platforms grew, they began to aggregate and automatically curate content with precision targeting based on the data they gathered on each user.

We gained potential readers when our articles were displayed. But these aggregated and targeted digital news magazines were also competitors. Aggregated content was free, taken without payment from the publications who paid to create it.

Worse, giants such as LinkedIn were also accumulating data on our audience which they could use for their own purposes. It appeared to be a conscious strategy. In the case of Google, where they once provided significant reader data based on our traffic, they stopped sharing this key data with us unless, of course, we agreed to become Google advertisers.

We were beginning to see how the new digital markets not only target market leaders but leaned towards monopoly leveraging Metcalfe's law. Once a player had a certain network size the value of that network made them impossible to ignore, even if leveraging that network forced you to contribute towards the growth of your own competitor. This competitor in turn, with a near zero and highly elastic cost structure leverages all aspects of the network towards building this new digital monopoly. In a digital world, this is the new flywheel and ultimately a virtually unstoppable force.

Even our 'non-digital' offerings were under siege. One of our previous employees developed CIO roundtable that targeted our customers with what was a duplication of one of our premium events. This added to competition from organizations from the U.S. and offshore parties, who increasingly were targeting Canada as an additional location for specialty events.

This new competition was particularly troubling in a small and limited market the size of Canada, both in terms of audience and in terms of the potential 'share of wallet' from our customer base. The new digital competitive landscape favoured the largest of the large who could achieve near monopoly status, and the small niche players or individuals who could operate with little in the way of overhead costs. It was tremendously unkind to mid-sized legacy organizations like ours.

Who was our competitor? Everyone. Individually we faced being crushed by the new giants or by the death of a thousand papercuts. Collectively, they were a fierce bear, one who, unlike the old joke, was insatiable.

We were in desperate need of a strategy. We needed to outrun the bear. That strategy would require us to first solve another key problem. We needed to rebuild our infrastructure quickly and with next to no budget.

Building an Agile Infrastructure

"Digital transformation is first and foremost a pursuit of customer experience. But in the digital world that customer experience cannot be fully realized without technology at its foundation. Consider it like building a house. Without the walls, the roof, the interior finishing, water, power, heat and lights – the 'experience' of the house would be missing. It would be unlivable. But without the foundation to build on, to hold it up and provide the services that sustain us, the house would be impossible.

So, it is with digital technology. We sought the agile enterprise to create the customer experience but found that our legacy foundation could not support the new structure. While we might aspire to be a luxury home, IT World Canada was at best a 'fixer-upper'.

- *Jim Love*

As noted earlier, the first few years of the Internet and the World Wide Web were a period of growth and experimentation for IT World Canada. Our first forays on the web were interesting and challenged the technology as it existed. The elevator doors of our first site were done purely with HTML and required complex overlays to create the effect. At the time, given the novelty of this new channel, we were perceived as pioneers. By today's standards, it would seem slow, awkward and embarrassingly simple.

Within a very few years the cracks started to appear. While we had grown enormously, that growth had been largely uncontrolled. Outside of the motif of the elevator there was little in way of any organizing principle or data architecture.

On the technical side, the company had been aggressive. In addition to the general business suite of applications email, accounting and CRM, the company had built or acquired several relatively sophisticated applications.

IT World Canada had a state-of-the-art email program from Europe. It hired outside contractors to build a custom content management system (CMS) based on the relatively new .Net framework. As online advertising grew, the company invested in a new ad server technology. When video emerged as a content type a new and expensive video platform was acquired. These alone would be significant for a company with less than a hundred employees, but there was more.

By 2010, the company had started two additional and extremely challenging projects. One of the projects was a highly customized version of SugarCRM.

The vision was to fully automate not only all sales and myriad administration processes but would also provide a new Audience Services subscriber database, integrated with the CMS. In addition, we had hired a consultant to create a new 'semantic analysis engine' for the CMS system to analyze and predict readers' preferences and serve them with targeted content. To say that the vision was aggressive would be an understatement. The size, the scope and the cost of these projects was enormous in comparison to overall revenue.

With increasing revenues and several government funding programs set to enable publishers to expand their digital offerings, the costs may have seemed reasonable. But when revenues started to decline the costs rapidly became unmanageable.

The move to discontinue print contributed to a huge drop in the company's top line revenue. At the same time, online advertising was becoming commoditized. The agencies who had once relied on us to be their preferred gateway to the IT decision maker were embracing the new ad networks and, in some cases, setting up their own trading desks. This made our agency customers quasi-competitors, pushing us even harder to prove the ROI of our unique audience.

While we attempted in the short run to focus more on our events business, which was one of the few that could still earn decent gross margins, we knew that this alone would not be sufficient to sustain us. In addition to events, our ability to create commercial content for our customers and amplify this on our own network was the best way to maintain our brand as a Canadian community builder. We needed to move from being a publisher to becoming a digital media business with new offerings that captured the zeitgeist of this new and emerging world.

All of this required a substantial investment in technology at a time when merely maintaining our existing systems was a challenge. Clearly, we needed a strategy to get ourselves out of this downward spiral. As we found so many times, it is hard to plan strategy when you are constantly kept off balance responding to the constant crisis of market demands on one hand and an aging architecture on the other.

This need to invest despite our losses was difficult, yet we knew it was the only decision. Meeting client demands for increased analytical reporting from online campaigns, webinars, lead generation and content as a service was essential to winning business. In addition to the need for increasingly granular reporting, we had an intense need for analytics to better understand the digital reader. The investment in technology to support the business plan was the biggest battle between the company's old and new shareholders.

Taking action in tech
The company had to become more competitive. Our technology, which should have enabled that competitiveness had moved from leading edge to legacy albatross. In the early days, we could paper over our technical failings. There are stories of late nights, long hours and at least one archetypal story about an executive who was forced to work every night to manually prepare promised reporting to a large client which our systems could not support. As the volume of work grew and with fewer staff, these 'Wizard of Oz' solutions were unsustainable.

We didn't have the flexibility to develop new products and every new client demand required significant manual intervention. Yet with declining revenue we also couldn't afford the costs of a large staff doing manual workarounds. We needed to automate the reporting that our clients were demanding.

We also needed better technology to serve our own needs for revenue growth. Our own digital marketing was non-existent, as all resources were focused on meeting the needs of increasingly demanding clients. Worst of all, our websites were showing their age. They were tired looking, in need of redesign and not able to keep up with the new demands for video and mobile content.

By the time Jim Love came to work for IT World Canada as a consultant, IT was caught in a cost squeeze. Essential projects that had been started such as revisions to the proprietary content management system (CMS) were on hold. A significant amount of our staff time was lost to firefighting, lurching from crisis to crisis. We ran our own admin systems including a mail server and phone systems, not uncommon in that day, but for the number of people we had it was tough to sustain. Basic infrastructure also often needed attention, as it had been implemented early and poorly. IT was expected to still provide Cadillac services, especially to the executives in the big offices that lined the windows and blocked out the daylight.

The grand projects such as the 'semantic engine' never worked. We had an enormous beast of a mailing system that we'd licensed from a Belgium supplier, which started as state-of-the-art but hadn't been updated in years. Only one person fully understood how to support it.

The CRM system was newer but the aggressive customizations to it had not been finished. The accounting system was not linked with any of the other systems and was not up to date. The audience management system although core to the business, remained unfinished and the staff were working with an old dBase tool and spreadsheets that required constant uploads and downloads.

The idea of 'one source of truth' was a foreign concept and data was processed in multiple locations with all the inaccuracy and confusion that this situation inevitably brings. Meetings broke down as two or more versions of the same data led to different conclusions and much debate.

To add insult to injury, most of our hardware was nearing the end of its usable life. We were running inefficient software on out of date and unreliable hardware. It was, in IT terms, the perfect storm.

All too common if truth be told
It would be easy to be critical of the IT systems, but truth be told, what had happened is neither new nor uncommon and if many companies were honest, they would admit to facing a similar situation. Perhaps theirs would not be as dire, but no one should take that for granted.

Like the proverbial iceberg, the problems often lie under the surface, as maintenance and upgrades are postponed in times of cost restraint. IT is often viewed as saviour or necessary evil, sometimes at the same time. This causes organizations to behave schizophrenically, lurching back and forth between aggressive development and equally aggressive cost management and cutbacks. In large companies this was epitomized by the phrase, "the CIO proposes, and the CFO opposes."

It was true that the company had been initially very aggressive in system development and adoption. It had great plans, most of which were overly ambitious. In fairness, some of the early developments, particularly on the web, were quite creative and leading edge. But there was a lot of learning going on as these were developed and the structure of many implementations was problematic. Moving forward without refactoring or restructuring these early experiments left a ticking time bomb in most of the systems.

Adding to the issues, instead of solidifying gains, we took on a massive number of projects, a workload which would have been ambitious for a company many times our size. Real governance and anything resembling a working level, let alone a strategic architecture, were ignored.

When the financial crunch hit, we tried to keep some projects running. Between firefighting and simply keeping the lights on we made little progress on these major projects. No matter how hard the team worked we showed little in the way of results. While fundamental issues took almost all maintenance time, we were further bogged down by a backlog of new requests from operations and clients alike.

It was the worst of both worlds. IT was still costing too much in terms of the company's revenue, yet we had too small of a team to balance the needs of running complex systems while sustaining ambitious projects with functionality that was over designed, unclear on the specifications and with no meaningful governance.

Through this chaos, senior IT, sales and operations staff who needed to work together to solve these problems were engaged instead in finger-pointing and often in open conflict. Much of this had more to do with positioning and politics than working on real solutions. Senior management were desperately looking for some way to control costs and had lost faith in any prospects of getting a real return on the technology investment.

Developing a strategy was going to be difficult. We lacked resources and we didn't get any breaks—breakdowns perhaps—but no real breaks.

The first few months of CIO Jim Love's tenure saw us lurching from one disaster to another. The CMS slowed down to an absolute crawl. This kept anyone from registering on a brand-new gating system that was to replace the old paper registration systems from the print days.

We spent night after night working on those issues even though, as we would discover, few people would register when the system was perfected. We barely got that system to a minimal workable level when another disaster struck. We were infected by a tenacious malware attack on our mail server. It took us more than a month to finally defeat the attack, which exploited the way the aging mail server and directory services had been implemented and once again, would have been less likely and easier to manage if those systems had been updated.

The CMS which was the heart of the new online content was a problem. The original contractors had done slipshod work. Everything was hard coded. There was no documentation to be found. The structure was convoluted and even experienced .Net programmers struggled with it. Simple changes would take forever although that was mostly a moot point since what little we had in the way of programming time was consumed by fixing errors. We had no resources to do any new work.

Not only was the CMS a programming and structural nightmare at the coding level, but the organization of content and the database structure remained unorganized and full of issues with broken links, missing data and other issues. That situation was further exacerbated by the growth in content over the years since the sites had been launched.

We had hundreds of thousands of pages on our sites taxing the performance and a convoluted indexing and menu system. With all that working against us, we had a phenomenal number of errors which impeded performance, threated to ruin user experience and endangered our ratings in search engines, most notably with the all-important Google algorithm.

Our ITWorldCanada.com site pages had so many errors that we exceeded the number that we could report with the tools we had to detect and log them. It was never clear to us why this system topped out after a hundred thousand errors, but it was the most that any of the team had ever seen on a production system so it is possible that the developers just never thought things would ever be this bad.

It was during these disasters that we gained an appreciation for the talent and dedication of the tech team. How they kept it all running and most of these issues from really impacting our audience was a tribute to their dedication and hard work. They worked, sometimes around the clock, during each the many crises we experienced. More than once we found someone sleeping on the couch in one of the meeting rooms, having worked all night on a problem.

The sad thing was that even with all of this incredible effort the divide between the 'business' and the 'tech' team continued to grow. Members of the sales team would rant about how awful the IT department in front of the same people who had worked all night.

With an abundance of problems, everyone wanted their urgent issue prioritized and those who could do so escalated at every opportunity. Failure to immediately drop what you were doing to respond was an affront to authority or a mark of the insensitivity of IT to business priorities. As we will see in the chapter *Culture* this was not restricted to IT but was part of the entire company's toxic culture. Nonetheless, it was demoralizing for the IT staff.

This feuding with IT was an immediate impediment to any progress with the IT crisis. The IT staff were making progress, but they were always in react mode since we were not addressing the root causes of problems. When we would try to focus on a systemic issue, the staff were constantly interrupted. This was simply unsustainable.

Over strenuous objections, we implemented work tickets and other monitoring systems that would support prioritization and root cause analysis. They would help us better understand the problems and try to be more efficient. As well, it was hoped that we would be able to show some progress and motivate the team to achieve even more.

We argued that if we were ever to make any progress, we needed to analyze and prioritize based not on emotion or the latest crisis but based on root cause and impact assessments. That logical and time proven strategy was presented and then thoroughly denounced by all as needless bureaucracy. Morale hit an all-time low.

Never waste a good crisis

Despite the resistance, it was clear that the only way out was to develop and implement a disciplined plan to turn things around. Most of the team had the skills to execute, they were just not able or allowed to think or act strategically. We couldn't simply bring in outside consultants. We didn't have the budget and we needed people who had knowledge or could dive deeper into the complexity of the problems we faced.

We identified two people who showed exceptional promise but lacked the experience to tackle issues of this magnitude. One was a talented manager in IT, a young man who led the hardware and infrastructure area but had not managed a development team. Second was a talented but young web designer who, although prone to rather immature reactions, was someone who had proven his ability to 'polish a turd' and get our systems to at least appear to meet some of the demands we faced.

We took the manager out of IT operations and put him working directly for the CIO and with Fawn as the business head we started building a plan to address not just the IT crisis but the financial crisis we faced. Central to that financial plan would be the restructuring and reworking of our entire IT structure.

We would take the added challenge that every positive structural change we made would have demonstrable financial benefits in terms of cutting costs. If we could align IT and show leadership in getting our costs under control, we would demonstrate the value of a disciplined approach.

Our case was simple. We needed a modernized, agile infrastructure to position us to make the necessary business changes to survive. In turn, we could leverage that to cut costs and increase efficiency but only if we did two key things.

First, we had to be bold and take some chances. Second, we needed a strong and disciplined execution which focused on root causes. There would be problems, but we would relentlessly focus on the strategic, at the expense of all but the most urgent tactical issues. We would adopt an agile approach, working in sprints to deliver measurable progress without attempting long term task level planning.

What we proposed was foreign to the organization. Like much larger organizations, people wanted familiar artifacts of planning—GANTT charts, milestones and fixed dates. We promised nothing of the sort. Our only promise was that we would show results.

We had only one trump card and we played this effectively, as we could simply not carry on the way were going. If someone else had a better plan to reduce problems in the long term, increase efficiency and cut costs, we were all ears. While we didn't promise dates, we backed up our plan with projected savings in real dollars.

The crisis proved to be our way past the inertia of departmental conflict and ineffective firefighting. But having won the day, we knew we had to show real results to quickly build confidence and to retain our ability to stay on plan.

The first thing we tackled was our aging hardware. While cloud and virtualization were relatively new, we would virtualize to create our own 'private cloud.' We dispensed with most of our old servers and centralized by virtualizing and making use of a fewer number of physical servers. We did find a deal and attractive leasing on some rack servers that could give us better, more reliable processing. We paid for these partly by consolidating from two higher priced hosting partners and aggregating under a smaller firm that gave us high quality at a lower price.

Using our motto 'never waste a good crisis' we leveraged every failure as an opportunity to make a change. Fresh on the heels of the mail server disaster, we took the opportunity to move to Google's new corporate mail service. It was relatively new and much cheaper than our internal systems, but the organization had been reluctant to lose its familiar and now traditional in-house system. Rather than trying to reengineer the old system, we simply ripped it out.

Instead of spending to maintain our aging on-site PBX we replaced it with a new VOIP system. We managed to override the concerns about quality from our owner by focusing on the difference in cost. He'd heard that VOIP had quality issues and in fairness, early implementations had been problematic. We were confident that we could do better. By showing how we would reduce our analogue phone bills and eliminate the maintenance costs on our PBX we made a solid case for change.

Once again, we selected a partner who could bring us creative ways to keep our costs low. There were some risks in going with a smaller provider, but our team did their homework very effectively. White board sessions with the vendor to develop solutions gave us a good impression of who would be the best bet.

This was supplemented by site visits and careful reference checking.

We encountered resistance at every step, working with new approaches, empathetic providers and moving systems offsite and out of our direct control. We also knew that we would have issues and we didn't hide that. We ensured that any plan clearly identified those we could imagine or possibly anticipate, immediately followed by a cost comparison and progress to our financial goals.

We did our best to reduce the impact of change. It took some work to learn the new Google setup, but we found creative ways to convert and structure our systems to allow us to continue to support the Outlook mail client, which a few of our more vocal users were passionate about keeping.

When push came to shove, when what we had implemented was new or different, we fell back on cost and reliability as our argument for everyone who chose to resist or argue. But we didn't go out of our way to create any more resistance than necessary. Often, to our surprise, the majority accepted the new world and even welcomed new tools and abilities. But a small but vocal group of critics remained, many of these in senior positions.

In that world, each new issue created tensions and threatened to derail our progress. We discovered weaknesses in the early cloud systems, some of which endure to this day. When our mail system developed problems for only a few individuals, we found out exactly how hard it is to get a cloud giant like Google to pay attention. We were only a tiny part of their client base.

Support from giants like Google was provided only via work tickets. The time required to get an issue resolved or even an explanation could easily extend into days. While this might be an annoyance to an individual with their personal email, when our staff complained that email issues were affecting sales or client service, we felt the pressure. Our great idea for cost saving could end up costing us revenue.

Likewise, we encountered issues on our phone system. While VOIP is simpler than running your own in-house PBX systems, when problems arise, they can be difficult to resolve. As luck (or Murphy's law) would have it, despite careful planning and execution, we had a lot of issues in the first days of our VOIP phone implementation.

Armchair quarterbacks abounded during every transition, and with every problem we faced the pressure from managers, the executive and even our major shareholder. While part of this could be attributed to the culture or the continuing divide between IT and business, in fairness, we were pushing the organization through a very rapid change. The amount of change was stressful for us all.

This is where our team showed their strength. Our former manager and now Director of IT, having overseen hardware and license support for years excelled at working with our suppliers. His own calmness under pressure and focus never wavered. He would spend time on the floor helping with even minor issues. His staff would likewise, under his coaching, spend hours on support lines. Our IT team, instead of demanding results or raising their voices, built relationships and showed either empathy or grim determination.

The team's ability to remain on hold was legendary. They did their homework, always 'consulting Dr. Google' and doing their research so as to be very well organized when looking for help from vendor support technicians. This strategy got results and occasionally got us an informal 'back door' to a helpful or sympathetic techie who could help troubleshoot or advise us.

They made progress and persevered, determined to make it work. When criticized, we pushed back with our argument that the status quo was expensive and unsupportable. Our motto, 'never waste a good crisis' was indeed paying off.

We could never have done this without the perseverance of our small but dedicated IT staff. They were determined and committed because we gave them tremendous autonomy when we made decisions. We let them do the investigations and to make the recommendations. They would select the approach and the partner we would work with.

This level of empowerment was new to this organization and even more difficult in today's world. It's a symptom of the modern era that end users are more sophisticated and are exposed to multiple solutions by vendors contacting them directly or increasingly by advertisements and email solicitations. Solution driven marketing communications inevitably describe a new product in glowing terms and focus on new features that are attractive to the user as they also expose the hidden limitations of their competitors.

As a company that specializes in technology journalism, and with a number of consultants striving to maintain their own relevance, we had this in spades. Every one of our decisions would be second guessed and questioned. There was always something better, always a new feature that our selected solution didn't yet have. Each would be an argument to change direction or the distraction of another 'add-on.'

We stuck firmly, perhaps even obstinately, to where the business areas could specify what they needed provided they could make a solid business case for the outcomes that would result from any investment of time or money. But for the first time, they were challenged to show how they would deliver measurable outcomes given the features they requested. When we didn't believe them, we still listened patiently. Even a broken clock is right twice a day.

But in the end, if we wanted savings and reliability, IT could be told *what* was required but not *how* the job was to be done. We would also be relentlessly focused on outcomes and not features; root causes and not symptoms or 'needs' not supported by a clear business outcome.

There were conflicts with our approach but ultimately, we won some victories along the way and gained at least a grudging acknowledgement of our credibility.

This approach carried over from the email and phone projects to a much larger and ambitious project. We proposed to replace the old .Net CMS system. We had some credibility here. Our early work had yielded savings and even grudging admission that what we had was more reliable. As well, we had facts and figures to back it up.

Our staff made prior projects work with few resources, small budgets and aggressive timelines. We might ask tough questions in the planning, but as a management team, we had to put our faith in them and support them through the inevitable implementation problems. We had, as we will note later in this chapter, found ways to fix a lot of the critical errors in the current CMS system. Despite that, what remained was inflexible and expensive to maintain. By the time we came forward with our plan, people were listening.

During these early days, it also became apparent that our new Director of IT had a real talent for negotiations. We let him take that on. He not only selected and dealt with new suppliers but managed to get better deals from our existing suppliers. He tackled our growing mobile costs. He reigned in spending on a multitude of items.

He also had the sense to not be 'penny wise and pound foolish.' He unwound some supposed previous cost savings done by barter and other arrangements. While these were initially low costs deals, they often cost us significantly in the long run. We had received some free licenses in a contra deal, but the support was so painful and took so many hours that he convinced us to buy new licenses despite the cost. We phased this in over time to reduce the impact and bit by bit we got past the painful 'bargain' that had been inflicted on us.

The strategy to build a small but strong and empowered IT group was paying off. As we moved forward, we got bolder.

We stopped development on a great number of fronts. We ripped out the old code from systems that would never deliver as promised. Even when we were certain, we didn't do this without serious and objective analysis. We did our homework.

For the semantic engine that was the brainchild of a senior consultant who had the ear of the owner, we invited the designer of the system in to explain his vision and design. We even paid him to do that at a time when dollars were short. After we had listened and truly tried to understand what would be required to make this system work, we successfully made the case to rip out the code, abandon the project and try to find a better way at some future point. Given that the initiators of the system were still working in the company and had considerable influence, we weren't sure we ever got formal approval, but clearly no one was going to directly oppose us. On this occasion, we took silence as consent and we didn't pursue and formal approval.

Admitting that a current project needs to be stopped is always difficult. There is a constant temptation to 'declare a victory and move on.' This is not a victimless crime. You may be able to save embarrassment by dragging a sick or dying horse across the finish line, but you never really win the race. It's still a sick or dying horse and it needs constant attention. That horse, in this case a system that would never work as promised, not only doesn't deliver championship results, it takes resources from other projects to preserve the fiction that it made it across the finish line.

In our case, not only would the ambitious and over-designed functionality never work, it interfered with performance and maintenance of the CMS system. We needed this code gone more than we needed a political fight.

We would wait for another day to make our case that the organization needed to be mature enough to openly accept that in some cases, in the greater scheme of things, some projects needed to be put out of their misery. Failure to admit failure only leads to more failure.

But we couldn't afford to have maintenance nightmares in our systems. We already needed to prioritize carefully, given our meager resources. Hard to maintain systems with constant issues were only part of our problem.

Another, perhaps even worse problem the organization had was that everything was an equal priority. IT was expected to drop everything and come running for even a minor problem. We could not support this. We had to find a way to logically prioritize and show that this would lead to better results.

We continued to insist on using our work request system despite strong opposition from the staff and much of the management. While it might feel like IT was more responsive in the old model, the reality was that this had a significant negative impact on productivity and quality of outcomes. The good old days of being able to interrupt anyone in IT had to come to an end.

Managing with the force of facts
We used measurement to make our case and to show success. Work requests now showed just how much it took to maintain the Cadillac service of the past. Logging requests and doing impact assessments took time, but the data and reporting allowed us to prioritize and look at root causes of multiple problems—not simply deal with individual complaints.

When we had successes, we had concrete data to show the results we were getting. This IT department had operated under the 'beatings will continue until morale improves' approach for too long. Finally, we could see and share real progress.

The new insights helped resolve long standing issues that truly threatened our business. Early in the game, we determined that our old CMS system had so many errors that the analysis software simply stopped working after it hit over a hundred thousand errors. We had no idea. Given that, everyone had simply thrown up their hands.

IT worked on other issues in a similar fashion— as they were raised with no idea or signs of progress. We could patch an individual page, but another error of a similar nature would surface almost immediately. While we played the technical equivalent of 'whack-a-mole' we knew that these broken links or problems with layout in articles were the result of underlying, unseen and systemic errors. These were the type of errors that would threaten our ranking on search engines, particularly Google, who was emerging as the absolute leader in this area.

We took one resource for a few days each week. He was freed up from firefighting to look for root causes. Our goal was simple. We needed to get our total errors to under one hundred thousand so that our analysis software would work, and we could finally get an accurate count of the errors and begin to show real progress.

This approach of measure and make progress had worked for us in other areas. People cannot be motivated if they cannot see and show progress. To achieve long term and ambitious goals, we need to see results. We applied this approach to this intractable problem.

We had to find some early wins to sustain this effort. We had to find and fix the root cause of the biggest errors. Our instructions to the programmer were clear. "Don't worry about the most critical errors unless the system is going to fall over. Look for the root cause of the greatest number of errors. Get the numbers down to where we can track them." We followed that until we celebrated a most unlikely achievement. We only had one hundred thousand more errors to fix.

Once we could report the number of errors, we showed them going down weekly. Our ability to show that finding and fixing root causes yields greater results was proven and becoming part of our new culture.

We followed the facts and refused to argue with every opinion out there. People still made their usual complaints about IT not being responsive, inevitably after someone had worked all night or all weekend but had failed to get to someone's individual request. But we had the data to counter their argument.

Equally important, when we had successes, we would tell the story at every opportunity. Statistics are important, but stories are remembered. The 'hundred thousand errors' story was told time and time again to illustrate that we could tackle big problems and win if we followed a disciplined approach of tackling the root causes and not the symptoms.

Despite the successes, we had a tough time convincing our IT staff to record and report. They expected that 'good work speaks for itself.' While that might be the way the world should work, nothing could be further from the truth.

We struggled to get them to follow our tried and true regime that learned from Lean practitioners and projects over the years. We had a clear and rigorous formula.

First agree how to measure the problem. Measure the prior state and get agreement on the fairness and accuracy of the method and results before you do anything in terms of improvement. If you wait until after the job is done, people will question how you did your calculations. If you agree on how to measure the current situation and what success is before you start, it's much harder to disagree with your reported success.

Use that same agreed on measure to consistently show progress and measurable results. Don't wait for the 'ultimate goal' to be achieved. Create and celebrate milestones to build confidence and retain commitment to the approach.

Using this approach, even partial successes must be acknowledged in terms of the outcomes they produce. We might not make all the problems go away but having most of what you sought to accomplish is still an accomplishment. Doing nothing because you can't fix everything is a one-way ticket to constant failure.

This last point is so important. Time after time, perfection gets in the way of results. We were told that we'd never get all the errors fixed. That might have been true. The last few thousand were tenacious and took a lot of work which we continued to do. But to have a few thousand versus over a hundred thousand is a massive accomplishment.

We pushed the staff hard to follow this formula in the same way that we had to push them to record and report. It was and remains a constant battle even though it worked when nothing else had. IT gained a reputation for slow but steady progress. Even those who wanted us to move more rapidly, were now grudgingly admitting our methods got results.

Our successes turned into stories and telling these gave us the needed credibility to achieve our goals. We didn't have big budgets or resources to tackle our problems. We had to find new and creative alternatives. We had to constantly ask if there was another alternative often to 'best practices' or what everyone else was doing. We were constantly looking to find an under-rated but still high-quality alternative.

We'd moved to Gmail when it was new and VOIP with a smaller partner. We scored a big victory when we replaced the very expensive video system used by our American counterparts with the emerging YouTube.

In the case of moving to YouTube, we hit the 'can't fix everything' syndrome again. We were challenged by one piece of missing functionality. YouTube didn't have the platform to let us sell pre-roll video segments. We were potentially going to incur a huge expense to only support one feature that we didn't currently sell.

We asked tough questions. How much pre-roll had we sold? How much would sales commit to if we kept the old system? How much could we make given those sales?

Once we did the numbers, in dollars and cents, we proved that we'd never pay for the expensive video system with the revenue we'd make even if pre-roll sales exploded. We proved that we could speak the language of business. We were focused on results and we expected everyone else to be. Likewise, we didn't hide behind technology. We focused on business results. When we finally did get a customer who requested pre-roll, we found an alternative.

Then came the point where we had the biggest test of our credibility. We proposed to stop fixing the current CMS system and replace it with an open source alternative—WordPress.

At that point, WordPress was credible but was still a risky alternative. There were a lot of questions. It could support blogs and some publications, but would it be able to do everything we needed at scale? Since it was open source, who would support it?

As we noted earlier, we were constantly approached with alternatives by companies that wanted to offer us a deal on their CMS and audience management systems. We had, at least for the present, won that war. No cost savings plan was enough to justify losing control of our database. We knew we would never give up our metadata to a third party that could analyze it and resell that knowledge.

We also had technical and cost concerns over the long term. When someone proposes something too good to be true, it often is. But our arguments were not technical. We focused on the business desire to protect the database.

We had all realized that our biggest asset was now our database and our knowledge of the community it represented. That was the source of our core value. The CMS and related audience information would stay firmly under our internal management.

So even with our small resources, we moved ahead with WordPress. In winning this point, our organization crossed a threshold. We were moving from tactical management towards a strategic governance that leveraged technology and valued intangible assets. We were making the first moves to becoming a digitally transformed organization.

Through that lens, we could see that our ability to understand our audience and to translate that understanding into engagement—audience experience—was our number one priority. Our ability to create and monetize that audience relationship was at the core of our business. Without them, nothing else mattered.

Our revenue, however, came not from the audience but from the advertisers who brought us revenue. Here again we needed to deliver an exceptional customer experience. To do that, we needed the systems and analytics to demonstrate the insights and success metrics that they needed. We had to find an alternative that we could do given our limited resources.

That was the basis of our decision to move to WordPress. After careful homework, we laid out a plan by which we could meet these goals and given our budgets, our skills and our team, it was the best alternative. Its low cost of ownership was a factor, but we looked realistically at all the issues including the key functions it would support and how it would integrate with our other systems. Once again, however, despite careful research, our decision was contested. Another consultant, again with the ear of the owner introduced another alternative.

We didn't argue on the technical merits. The proposed alternative, Drupal, was credible and also open source. Our team had considered it and rejected it for various reasons. We didn't argue those. We argued that we needed to back our team who we needed to pull together and against the odds, get us the new CMS we desperately needed. Having achieved a certain sense of accomplishment and reputation, however, we took this challenge not as a threat, but as a legitimate testing of our decision. What a quantum leap that was for our group. We were no longer under siege; we were being appropriately tested.

We made our case. We had to be realistic. We had a tiny team regardless of talent and determination and we were building and converting a massive system with over a hundred thousand or more pages. They had to be fully engaged and motivated. While Drupal may have merit, the team was committed to their direction. They would make it work.

That argument, more than anything else, won the day. We began the project.

We moved our sole open source programmer from the failed audience services project. We took our young designer who knew enough to be dangerous about PHP (the open source programming language that WordPress is written in) but was eager to experiment and learn. We put these under the management of our Director of IT, who had a lot of experience with hardware but had never run a development project or conversion project of this size and complexity. The team had worked hard and proven themselves on other projects, but this was still a large risk.

A lot of companies were using WordPress. How many companies had moved a site with this many pages and countless lines of custom code? We were risking not just the functionality. We were also taking a risk with our Google ranking, something that had taken us years to build.

We weren't done. We added one more piece to the puzzle. We were going to do this without building a mobile app. We would embrace an emerging idea called 'responsive design.' Under this new approach, our site would anticipate and adjust to every device, tablet, phone, laptop or desktop.

Minimum Viable Product

We knew that this was a high-risk project, especially for an organization that had over-reached many times in the past and failed.

Failure is a unique thing in a corporation. The known adage is that 'you only learn from your failures' is wonderful in theory, but in reality, companies hate failure and despite any claim to the contrary failure is punished, not rewarded. It might not be overt, you might not be dismissed or demoted, but there is a penalty for failing.

This leads to a universal phenomenon. Failures are hidden, ignored or minimized. If they are discussed at all, it is most often part of an effort to divert, rationalize or shift the blame. They are not openly and honestly discussed. Because of this, we only learn one lesson from our corporate failures and that is, "don't try that again."

The stigma that we attach to failure acts like a vaccination against future attempts to take risks or try new ideas. It builds an immune system that kills new ideas. IT World Canada was no exception. The answer to every new idea was all too often "we tried that before and failed."

We had the 'luxury' of having no other option. The current CMS, despite our hard work to fix errors, was at the end of its useful life and would be an insurmountable barrier to our further progress. We couldn't meet demands for new services. We could never deliver the type of user experience that we needed to survive competitively, particularly in the mobile world. Further, the cost of maintaining the current system was not supportable.

We argued that any strategy would have some risks. But no matter how we stacked it, with our staffing, experience and budget, not to mention the data and structural issues on the old system, our plan to construct and convert to a new system was very high risk.

Our challenge was this. How did we fully acknowledge the risks and still get the buy in to move forward with this project? Our answer was simple and honest. We might indeed fail, but if we did, we would make the failure fast and manageable with time to find another alternative.

We proposed that we would build a prototype, using an approach common to start-ups and referred to as minimum viable product (MVP). The MVP is a way of getting a system that functions just well enough to allow you to find out how actual customers will react to the new system and features. It may not do everything, but it proves the basic value and practicality of the idea. It also rapidly creates something that you can use to involve and observe customer interaction. This approach is at the heart of many successful start-ups and more than a few unicorns.

Our use of this differs somewhat from what has been written about the MVP. It's often treated as a very early 'dare to be bad' prototype and in one version, referred to as the 'Wizard of Oz,' as the functionality may be manually bridged. You can get to the essence of what is really important or engaging without building all of the functionality that a production version should have.

We needed more. We had to understand the user experience, but we also needed to prove the 'V' in MVP. We needed to make sure that we provided not only a great experience for our readers, but that we also proved the ultimate technical viability of our project. It had to function at scale and preserve our search engine ranking.

We did stay true to the core of the MVP approach. We would not draft a large list of specifications, have design meetings and follow the steps that led to the overdesign of systems in the past.

We would have a balance. Our first generation might not be perfect, but it would be appealing to an audience. It would work well enough to allow us to evolve it with our audience, our editors and our staff. It would prove that we could convert our sites with tens of thousands or more pages to the new format and retain our Google search ratings.

We decided that we would take our smallest publication, a French language site called *Direction Informatique*. We would use that to prove our approach. If we were going to fail, that was a small enough audience to allow us to 'fail fast' and if necessary, recover quickly.

While this meant building more structure than might be associated with an MVP, it still skirted the traps of the past. Not only did we want to avoid over-design, but we could not afford a classic approach with large and detailed specs. Nor could we drop everything and divert all resources to the new systems.

While we did consult with business users, we kept our stubborn insistence that we maintain our agile approach. For us, this was taking the irritating position of steadfastly refusing to give dates but regularly releasing packages that had real value to the user.

We focused on user stories driven by what we called the 'agile question.' For any function or feature we would ask who the person was who wanted this and why they wanted it. What would they do and why? It forced us to break away from the huge wish lists of the past. It focused us all on the experience of the reader or the direct user of the system. On every whiteboard in the company you would at one point or other see this written:

> You want this (function) _____ so that you can do this _____ (measurable business result).

We acknowledged that we didn't have the resources or budget to do everything. We would select some key use cases. We would prioritize based on expected outcomes, not our own preconceived ideas.

The approach worked. For example, if we had asked the business users directly, they would have correctly indicated that mobile user experience was essential to any new CMS. The next logical conclusion for them is that we must develop a mobile app. We had this actual discussion.

Yet we knew from experience and a realistic self-assessment that we were in no shape to develop and support mobile apps for every platform that our readers used. We had iOS, Android, phones and tablets and yes, even BlackBerry was still a major part of our audience. Even if we could develop for all those platforms, even if we could restrict our support to a few generations of each operating system, we would still fail. If we lived through development, we'd die in support and maintenance.

Instead we took the strategy proposed by our young designer not to develop mobile and tablet apps. We would implement 'responsive design.' In theory—as there were few fully developed applications out there—we could design the CMS in such a way that it would allow us to intercept the request, tell what size screen you were communicating from and then serve a view that would fit that device. That was the goal. In the initial version or MVP, however, we were happy to merely have screens that, when collapsing into a smaller form factor, would do so in a way that preserved a coherent and workable design. The rest could come later.

Responsive design also fit one of the non-negotiable architectural principles that we insisted on, which was the separation of the presentation layer from the underlying storage and processing. We had adopted the idea of architectural principles early in our planning. To avoid building a system that moved straight from implementation to legacy wasn't done by adding more and more functions. We could only future proof our decision process by focusing on a handful of key principles that would guide us to preserve the foundations of longevity.

Open standards were one of these. No system can do it all. We needed to ensure that we could add on and communicate with other modules and even systems if needed.

The second key architectural principle was that the content and functionality must be separate from the presentation. We knew that the look and feel of our sites would be in constant change. If we had to change the core logic when we wanted to change how the system presented the content, we'd be back to square one with an instant legacy.

Our third principle was applicable to the responsive design decision. It stated that we must be able to support all current and future mobile devices, as well as all their supported operating systems and versions.

We felt responsive design was absolutely the way to go. It fit our architectural principles. It had a great case for long term support. But it was brand new and not every problem had been identified, much less solved. We would eventually beat those issues but at this point, having not built anything other than early prototypes, we didn't know what we didn't know.

As we made our case that this was the right approach, we caught a small break. Twitter had adopted responsive design. This gave us one more piece of evidence to support our direction. We might have problems, but we were much surer we could scale this if Twitter was adopting this approach.

In the months that followed others would make similar choices, but by that point our small but mighty crew would be months into the project and have found and beaten each challenge we faced. Even when we got to the migration of the larger systems and faced a host of problems with the data structures and conversion, they never lost faith and always found a solution. They delivered a functioning CMS that was a hit with our readers containing all the functionality needed in record time.

Had we made all the right choices? We were never sure. What we were certain of was that our team owned the 'how' decision to find a way to solve whatever challenge faced them. Yes, we would make mistakes, but we would make them early so that we could discuss them openly and learn. Given that, if anyone could make it work, this team would do it, and they did. Even if everything wasn't just as we envisioned it, our business and our customers would get the key outcomes they needed.

End state

In the months following our launch of the new WordPress based CMS we went to a conference in Boston which featured publishing companies from around the world owned or partnered with IDG Group, our minority shareholder and partner. When our designer Jeff Radecki was asked to make a presentation on responsive design and how to make it work, we knew we'd crossed a threshold.

We had cut our IT spending in half. We had modernized the infrastructure so that we could do the things our clients were demanding without massive hard coding. We had built an agile infrastructure to deliver our digital content. We were doing leading-edge design.

The CMS implementation was a milestone in terms of technical progress, but also a landmark in our cultural change. IT was no longer the scapegoat. IT had gained real credibility and was now core to the strategy of the organization. We wouldn't accept 'we tried that before and failed.' Failure was a necessary step on the way to success. Everyone failed and the business fiction that refused to admit this was idiocy. We were no longer playing that game.

When we went on to fix the audience management system and even eventually our troubled CRM, we knew we'd win despite the odds. Admitting and addressing failure out in the open makes you stronger. In the months that followed we would apply what we had learned to the operations and the cultural change needed to the entire organization.

We had successfully built an agile and affordable digital infrastructure. We had made IT a clear partner for the business. Lastly, we had the blueprint to build a culture of success. Through these trials and tribulations, we now had a component of what we needed to compete in the digital publishing world.

Culture

"When the change you want to make conflicts with your current corporate culture, you have three options. Option one - change the culture. That is very, very hard and takes years. Option two is change the change. Do something different that doesn't require cultural change. What's option three? Simple. Prepare to fail."
- Daryl Conner, author of Managing at the Speed of Change

It's been more than three decades since the idea of Organizational Change Management (OCM) was introduced to focus on the human side of technological change in organizations. Since that time the approaches and methods have matured. There have been many advances, a great deal of learning, and a large amount written by brilliant authors and practitioners.

In all this time, no one has found a way to solve the challenge of cultural change presented by Daryl Conner. When everything else is done—education, training, persuasion, compensation, communication—culture remains the greatest barrier to change.

Culture by its nature is the ultimate roadblock for those trying to achieve radical change. It represents the aggregate of how people internalize a shared view of the organization. It acts to preserve that vision of the company including its processes, its formal and informal structures, the business model, the values and every other aspect of the shared world that is the organization.

That is the conundrum. For truly radical change to happen, one must change the culture. Yet culture resists change because it exists to preserve the company as it is. As a result, it takes time and enormous effort to change corporate culture. For those trying to create agile organizations, it has proven to be the ultimate challenge. For many, it has been the hill on which the battle is lost.

There have been numerous strategies that companies have tried to use to speed up cultural change. One is simply to ignore it as a factor. Focus simply on changing processes and be brutal about implementation. Do not take no for an answer. In the old days we would refer to this approach as 'kick ass and take names.' Those who attempt this have an illusion of progress, at least initially, but are surprised and frustrated when, after much work and effort, the new processes have an uncanny resemblance to the old. New names remain and a few new steps are retained, but the same rigidity and inefficiency creeps back in. Or even worse, you get malicious compliance where your instructions are executed with the realization that they may even have disastrous consequences. When problems occur, the staff can say, "we are just obeying orders."

To change any process, you must make lasting changes to behaviour. To change behaviour, even if you have all the skills, the training and the information to be able to make a change, you must also find or create a willingness to change. Such is the challenge companies have faced throughout our modern history. You can have a great strategy to change your organization, but as the saying goes, 'culture eats strategy for breakfast.'

Digital transformation adds yet another layer of complexity. To achieve the agility that is inherently needed by these organizations, an even more radical change to the organization culture is required. Not just those who do the day to day work of the organization, but also those who run and lead the organization must change. Management culture must also be driven to change.

Hierarchical control, the way we have run the modern organization since the first models of modern corporate management were developed, is simply not workable in a digital organization. It is far too slow and rigid to meet the challenges of the hyper-competitive, customer centric digital world. We need to find new ways to lead and guide the organization.

To respond quickly enough to deliver on customer experience, to innovate and to implement in real time requires a high degree of autonomy for the employees. For any organization more than ten years old, this is a huge change and verges on the impossible.

All of us have experienced an encounter with the large corporation that forces everyone to accept their bureaucratic process with the employee as slave to the corporate rules. We've seen that sheepish look where they agree that our complaint is valid but are powerless to help. It's frustrating for them and us. In the electronic world, what is the impact of this rigidity when the customer is only a click away from a new supplier?

Not only can companies not serve existing customers, they cannot innovate and create new products and services quickly enough in a hierarchical, controlled environment. IT World Canada in an interview asked Werner Vogels, CTO of Amazon, how AWS was able to bring over 90 new services to market in a little over a year. His answer was unequivocal. "We couldn't have developed this quickly with standard hierarchical systems of management."

In this light, we all love to talk about flat and agile organizations. Many will nod when the topic is raised. The reality is that a non-hierarchical and flatter organization, one which gives people autonomy is frightening to those who must manage, or rather, lead an organization. How can they retain some level of control, some way of ensuring that everyone is moving in the same overall strategic direction?

The answer is to marshal the force that works. Use culture. The agile organization required to support digital transformation forces us to do the most difficult type of change, at an accelerated pace, but it uses culture to ensure that everyone moves in the same direction.

Cultural change takes time. It also requires a level of leadership that few companies can muster. In digital transformation, employees need to change, and their journey is difficult. But the real barrier is found in the management that refuses to change their style and even beliefs about leadership.

There are leaders who are blind to the necessity for change. There are those who are slow to realize the change is coming and ignore the issues until the point where change is forced too quickly on the organization. By that time, the company may be so severely disrupted, it now lacks any hope of being able to transform quickly enough. When that happens, the leadership and the organization sit like a deer in the headlights, waiting for the oncoming collision. We could not afford to let that happen.

The myth of the strong leader

Cultural change requires strong leadership and in digital transformation that leadership must not only lead the change – but they must also change themselves. They must acknowledge that in digital transformation what was your core strength becomes your key weakness. Your legacy of success holds you back. The culture that made you so successful is only doing its job, functioning like an immune system, fighting back against outside influence.

Before we can fix this problem, we must change how we see it. Humans are pre-programmed to find and retain patterns of behaviour. In individuals, these are habits and beliefs. In groups and organizations, this is the culture. It's neither good nor bad.

An organization needs a culture to regulate it. Resistance to change is not a lack of intelligence, or commitment, and it's even desirable in some cases. In many circumstances, those who are difficult to change are precisely those who in the past have been relied on to keep an organization on track and defend its core values. In other cases, those who are easy to change may lack discipline or resolve or easily be taken off track. Those who are most resistant may be our top performers who have not yet realized that our expertise and intelligence is often what is holding us back.

Traditional approaches to cultural change will not work. You can't use rewards and punishment or the so-called 'carrot and stick' approaches. Punishment drives resistance underground. Neither can a purely intellectual appeal work. Culture operates at a deeper level.

Cultural change requires nothing less than a new way of seeing things. In the world of digital transformation this goes to the core of all our beliefs learned in legacy organizations, including the way we manage them. Our organizations are not merely aggregations of physical assets, computer systems, processes and locations. If that's all we see, then we are blind to the expertise, the knowledge the beliefs and structures that bring life to our commercial abode.

In the new digital or digitally enabled company we can add three additional key elements, namely, authenticity, values and purpose. In our experience only a culture that enables these three elements can be agile enough, empathetic enough, flexible enough and ultimately inspiring enough to enable an organization to meet the challenges we will face in the coming years. Changing this is a tall order, changing it rapidly enough is even more difficult. Yet even for large companies, failure may not be an option.

Late recovery – not always an option

In the early days of digital disruption some large companies were slow to react due to their culture. That they didn't fail is largely attributed to the resources they had to make up for those missed opportunities. Even under the genius of Bill Gates, Microsoft missed the advent of the Internet and let upstart Mozilla and later Netscape dominate in the new world of browsers.

Microsoft had the resources to play catch up. They simply gave away their browser bundled in their software. Was it inferior to Netscape? Absolutely. But with the money and the installed base of customers, Microsoft would dodge the bullet.

Microsoft then went on to miss the impact of Linux and the world of open source software. Later they were incredibly late to the Software as a Service (SaaS) market. Some would claim that they also entered the hosting market with Azure much later than they should have.

In each case, Microsoft has somehow found the time and resources to play catch up. In a number of cases, like music, home entertainment, the tablet and the mobile phones, they did fail, and could not recover. But given their size, they were able to quietly abandon those areas and often huge investments and focus on other places they could succeed. If you are that rich and that embedded in the ecosystem, with that many alternate directions, you might be able to afford to make mistakes. Today, however Microsoft, under the leadership of Nadella is making bold moves to flatten the structure and change the culture realizing that even for a giant like Microsoft, playing catch up is a dangerous game.

If you are large enough, you can also employ the strategy of buying your emerging digital competitors. This has become so prevalent that start-ups count on this as their 'exit strategy.' If a start-up can innovate and irritate a much larger rival by taking even a portion of their business, they will offer to buy you. Poke the bear enough to make him mad enough to buy you at an inflated valuation. It's been done repeatedly.

For some, the world is not so kind, and neither strategy works despite their size and resources. Kodak was cognizant that digital photography was an issue that could endanger their business. Vince Barabba, a former Kodak executive openly shared the fact that the company knew about the impending threat for many years. Kodak commissioned a study that accurately predicted it had ten years to deal with digital photography. It continued to do research, but ultimately over the ten years, it did little. When it did finally awake to the threat, it was too late.

The strategy of wait and play catch up or buy your disruptor is no guarantee of success, even for large and wealthy companies. In fact, the list of large companies that couldn't play catch up is much, much longer than the list of those who survived.

Kodak, Blockbuster, Sears - the list goes on and on. It wasn't that these companies were not innovative in their time. Each of them had at one time been a formidable disruptor. But once they had achieved giant status, their culture made them blind to new threats. Further, that cultural 'immune system' viciously attacked anyone who dared to point out the need to change. The reality is that all too many companies, big and small, do not have cultures that enable them to react quickly, taking courageous action while there's still time.

Make no mistake, responding to digital disruption can only be described as courageous. If it develops a digital alternative, a company is competing with or cannibalizing its own products. Which manager or product leader will have the vision to sacrifice their current product line and possibly their status and compensation to nurture a new internal competitor? Which leader wants to go to their investors and explain how they are attacking their own products in favor a new and unproven alternative where the market may be several years out? In a world where we reward risk avoidance and continuous reliable economic growth there are real reasons why defending the status quo instead getting behind an uncertain future offering would be a rational strategy.

Still, ignoring a problem in one fiscal quarter knowing that you could see earnings plummet in the next three to four quarters is not rational. Nor does it fulfill the mandate to create long term value for shareholders. No board of directors or group of shareholders would vote for this option if they saw and believed they were exchanging short term reliable earnings for medium to long term disaster. Unfortunately, digital disruption offers no certainty as to the timing and impact of the disruption or of the company's ability to respond and survive. Historically, some large companies have survived many mistakes. Others have fallen because of one serious misstep. That's the challenge.

No one can promise investors and management when the digital threat will hit with full impact. No one can promise that their strategy to transform will be successful. Everything in business has a risk. Everything in digital transformation has a bigger risk. Ultimately, this is where the primary struggle with company culture occurs. Corporate cultures, especially for those who dominate their industry, function to reduce risk and to preserve, not destroy what has been built.

This is why digital transformation is difficult from a leadership and a cultural standpoint. For an executive, taking action requires courage in the face of uncertainty. There are huge risks involved whether you move forward or stand still. The only certainty is that you will make mistakes and will need to rapidly assess, recover and even change direction.

One problem is that the ability to learn and foster change, cannot, or perhaps should not be borne by a single individual. It should be embedded within a team and even within the culture. That's when it keeps the company on track, while still allowing it to take risks, to acknowledge failure, to learn and rapidly recover. That is exceedingly rare.

The few leaders who have taken their companies back from the brink have focused not only on their strategy but on their culture. John Chen at BlackBerry, Satya Nadella at Microsoft, and others who have brought change to their organization have focused not on a cult of leadership, but on building a culture that can execute the company's vision and still challenge the status quo when it counts. Werner Vogels, the legendary CTO of AWS considered his job to be developing and maintaining a culture that made the accomplishments that have allowed AWS to dominate the industry in relatively few years.

It is possible to change. It is possible to build a culture that can enable you to adapt and even prosper in an era of digital disruption. But it's one of the hardest things to do.

Dysfunction and success

If you came to the offices of IT World Canada at the time we stopped printing in 2011 you might be shocked by what you saw. A few short years before, there would have been a hundred plus people buzzing around to get the various print publications out. Journalists would be writing stories for print and posting to the various websites. The fledgling video studio would be producing interviews for the web. People would be working on logistic and visuals for large government events like Lac Carling and Showcase Ontario.

In its early days, IT World Canada, at that time called Laurentian Technomedia, experimented and grew rapidly. That was what attracted a young Fawn Annan to join the company—the opportunity to work with Andy White and IT World Canada and in 1995 to create and lead an executive division with CIO programming. Andy was looking for an out-of-the-box thinker and doer, with proven entrepreneurial success. A one-year contract led to a twenty-four-year tenure for Fawn.

But even at that point the culture of the organization had a dark side. The culture was top down, authoritarian and highly political—what has been described as an 'old boys club' run with a strong authoritarian streak. It mirrored the top-down culture prevalent in IT in the early days combined with the worst of the journalistic cultures that we have all seen in movies and on TV.

It didn't take long for someone new to see that although there was a very formal management structure, it was truly an 'owner operated' company where the CEO and owner had the final word on all decisions. In response, management at the time played the game of flying 'under the radar' and trying to move things forward without drawing the owner's attention. That second level was in turn equally a top-down authoritarian sub-culture, where power resided with the president and the editor-in-chief. The instruction from the president was clear. "Don't go above anyone's head."

IT World Canada's authoritarian culture perpetuated a world of the zero-sum game. There were always winners and losers. If someone won, someone else had to lose. One of the issues we saw over and over was that if projects or products were moved to new people there were conflicts with the previous 'owner.' Mostly these were covert, although sometimes these were overt and led to angry exchanges.

There were outbursts and strained relationships in the office. Those who avoided this open conflict fell into the morass of backroom behind the scenes politics. The culture was aptly described as 'bitchy, underhanded and highly political.'

Why did people stay? Despite the protectionism around information and product ownership; the lack of sharing knowledge; the political games played; there remained the excitement of the challenges of building and creating that compensated for the negative aspects of the culture. For many of the writers and the other talented people who came through our doors the challenge of the work overcame the negative aspects of the culture. You kept your head down, you tried to stay out of executive combat and in return got to work on the projects you enjoyed or that were truly leading edge—or both.

To many who worked at the company, the owner, although charismatic and able to make fine speeches at internal corporate gatherings, seemed oblivious to all the exceptionally talented people who truly tried to make a difference through their work. He was the hero of the story. The rest felt like they were 'the help.' Despite some sentimental loyalties to long serving and non-threatening individuals, the rest were 'replaceable.' He would most likely be mortified to hear this but to those who worked for him it was a truth that they would only admit privately.

Despite the problematic culture the company had been extremely successful. The owner had built a chain of publications and businesses and was a successful entrepreneur. The first president complemented the owner with a mixture of drive and imagination, combined with a burning ambition to be number one in the market. The British editor-in-chief was a seasoned engineer and IT specialist with a deep knowledge of the industry.

Under this regime the company became number one in the IT publishing world in Canada culminating in the acquisition of its main competitor. It forged an agreement with the international publishing giant IDG and with that, gained the ability to use its brands in Canada including the CIO brand for its flagship publication. It had huge prominence in the Canadian market from its publications and its events. It was successful.

Signature events such as Lac Carling—which involved the federal, provincial and municipal governments across Canada helped build the overall executive brand. It produced for twelve consecutive years, Showcase Ontario, a huge event hosted annually by the Ontario government. These events were phenomenally challenging, but also highly rewarding in terms of serving a real purpose of community and having a huge impact, making a difference in the advance e-government. These activities were also very successful commercially. The government division, and these events at their height were responsible for almost a third of our revenue.

Yet, underneath it all the IT World culture was unquestionably corrosive, misogynistic and for some, toxic. This face was never seen by the outside world. Somehow the company not only masked its flaws externally, but also remained very successful and highly regarded in the industry. This was possible when growth and increasing revenues allowed it to hide such flaws. When revenue started to decline and new challenges emerged, the organization stumbled badly, and the cracks were showing.

The office in 2011 was a different world. It had been shrinking for some time, but now there was empty space everywhere. Although it had clearly fallen in terms of size, the old structure was still apparent. To someone from a more modern environment, it would feel like taking a step back to the 1970's. In the center of the office, away from the windows, were the 'workers' in their cubicles, heads down and hard at work. Each group sat in their own area. Operations was separate from creative services. Sales had its own clique. Editorial was in its own group because of 'church and state' philosophies. IT was off in the corner.

Along the windows on the outside of the building were the executive and management offices with large integrated wood furnishings, white boards, screens. For those who were senior enough there were tables for meetings in the office.

There were two large corner offices. One was now a meeting room, with a tribute to the now deceased president Andy White on the door. The other was a large corner office with its own waiting room where the owner's personal assistant sat guarding the door. It was clearly a power symbol, right down to having its own boardroom table and washroom.

Another remnant of the old culture remained. The combativeness and highly political nature reigned supreme. Sometime after Andy White died, the role of president was given to Fawn Annan but only after the male heir apparent left after a conflict with the owner to pursue a digital photo business he had been running on the side.

By that time, Fawn had done every job in the company and was clearly the only one with the expertise and skill to move the company forward. Yet, without consulting his new president, the owner immediately undercut her authority and hired a combative and aggressive Vice President of Sales, who immediately began his own war with the IT group and, it was rumored, was looking to leverage that to oust Fawn as president.

The company had changed and yet much had remained the same. Yet the cracks were beginning to show. Although it was not yet losing money, revenue had declined considerably. The company remained incredibly siloed.

Each department had an issue with another. Sales thought that Editorial was out of touch. Editorial thought that Sales were a bunch of yahoos that didn't respect journalists. Audience Services felt they got little respect and support. Operations people felt unappreciated.

The shrinking creative services department had no time for creative work and when challenged to be more creative, they complained that they were on an assembly line. The SEO and analytics area produced a multitude of information and reports that nobody used effectively. In response, they continued plans and projects to increase SEO activities that no-one implemented in the operation.

There was only one true unifying factor—everyone thought IT was doing a crappy job.

The business was changing. But the remnants of the old culture stubbornly held on, only now that old culture was a huge impediment to addressing the challenges that the company faced—and there were major challenges.

In addition to the revenue challenges, the cracks in the organization were showing. System development was in trouble. Projects were lagging and producing little in the way of results. The company could not adapt to the new products and demands of customers.

Finding someone to lead the company through its technology challenges was essential. We had some good people but having lived in command and control structure for so long they were unable or unwilling to think strategically, nor did they have the experience to lead our technology development through this tough time.

The culture fights back

We always assume that leadership of change must come from the top. Yet many times leadership happens at all levels of a company. In our case, one of our leading consultants, David Jonah, who had been our 'guru of measurement' and who had become a friend and quiet supporter of Fawn's presidency went outside the organization and brought in a consultant to tackle the system issues. With David's support, Jim Love was brought in to try to solve the technology issues. Shortly after that, Fawn would appoint Jim as acting CIO.

David knew that he wasn't the one to take the company through the changes it needed. David recruited the person who he thought would supplant him, even though he privately confided to Fawn that he knew that there was room for only one person leading the strategic and operational technology. In effect, he sacrificed his own opportunity for the good of the company—a textbook example of leadership.

The change that was required would not be easy. The organization and its old-style hierarchical culture had built many strategies to resist change. For example, as our new CIO challenged people to think in new ways the response would be "if you knew our industry, you'd understand." Or there would be the finger pointing. "We'd be okay if only that other department would do their job right." Inevitably, there was the 'blame IT' excuse.

The VP of Sales' first meetings with the new CIO launched into a profane tirade where in response to an innocuous question, he blustered that he'd already told IT everything and he wasn't repeating himself. To him the number one problem with the organization was that IT was stupid, incompetent and wouldn't listen. It was leadership in reverse.

When we dove into it, we found that people had adapted to dysfunction. They didn't know this was wrong or even what a positive culture was like. They did make their own fun at gatherings and parties and in those cases the exchanges were pleasant and positive. As little as a few hours later, or even at the same event, the gloves would come off or the knives would come out.

More than anything, the organization had developed a culture of defeatism. 'We tried that before and it failed' was the answer to any new suggestion. It's a hallmark of hierarchical cultures with punishment for mistakes. It's also indicative of a culture that doesn't execute.

The company had learned to fail. As we have noted earlier, one of the worst things that a management group can do is to start a project or initiative and just let it die quietly or pretend a failure was a success. When you do that, you teach an organization that 'this too shall pass' is a valid strategy. If something is failing, you don't have to keep it alive. But you must openly acknowledge that it was failing. Equally, you need to look at the reasons for the failure without ascribing blame. Without that, the culture will evolve to incorporate this dysfunction and where possible avoid the issue altogether by never taking risks.

The best organizations adopt a 'can-do' attitude that we strove for as we attempted to change this toxic and defeatist culture. 'There is no shame in failing,", we said. "There is only shame in not learning." This is easy to say, but hard to instill in a company whose culture is based on finger pointing, blame and conflict. Nevertheless, it is a fight that must be fought and won.

Lack of learning, failure to persevere in adversity and quietly burying failures all lead to the same outcome. They teach the organization how to fail. They inoculate against change. They embed resistance so that it functions like an immune system, destroying new ideas and reinforcing the idea that change is not possible.

The IT World culture lost some of its overt toxicity with the move of Fawn Annan to the president's role, but it retained the worst aspects of its culture and a steadfast inability to objectively analyze and address issues. This was even more ironic, given that the organization excelled at analytics. The company amassed a huge amount of data without ever becoming a 'data driven' culture. The only use for the data that it gathered was to support existing opinions, making key decisions on miniscule data and frequently turning a single isolated number into a trend.

This was the culture of the company. It had over the years accumulated almost every cultural problem that an organization could have as an impediment to change. If one clearly looked at the data, an objective person would realize the company was in dire trouble and not just financially. If it was to survive these issues had to be addressed. Financial success masked the cultural dysfunction. In the current world of declining revenue, it no longer could be hidden or denied.

We might seem like we are painting a bleak picture or even denigrating the organization. Speaking honestly, many companies today are in a similar state. At the time when they most need to be resilient, when you pull the covers back, there is a tremendous amount of resistance to change and dysfunction baked into the culture. It's essential to address, but to do that, first you must see it and acknowledge it. We were determined to do just that.

The weeks, months and eventually years were filled with difficulty as we tried to move forward. We couldn't address everything, but we could shine a light on problems by leveraging data and focusing on facts. We pushed relentlessly for objective data and steadfastly refused to accept opinions masquerading as truth. If there was a problem, we insisted on gathering the facts and doing impact assessments and root cause analysis.

We needed to break the prison of the hierarchical, command and control culture that we had inherited, which seemed so difficult to obliterate. Although we were benign dictators, we were still a command and control organization. We too could be part of the problem. When we would regress into this, we'd remind ourselves that change starts with the leadership. In later years, senior staff would firmly remind us when we veered offside of the culture that we spent such enormous effort to build.

There were and have been victories. We have seen the new behaviours emerge and celebrate these when they do occur.

Some things remain a puzzle. Remarkably, our attempts to flatten the organization weren't as welcomed as we thought. We continually hear how employees and companies embrace a flat structure, but we found that many employees in our case were confused and stubbornly clung to hierarchical structures, titles and symbols of status and authority.

This created a real issue when we downsized our premises. We had to confront the problem of too few offices which meant removing or sharing offices. We knew that of all the things that you can do to an employee, taking away status is one of the worst things possible. That's why a flat structure makes a company so much more agile. Level or status doesn't get in the way of change. But we were not there yet and any move to change who had offices or to force people to share them was going to be contentious.

It was at this point that we had a brilliant idea. We became the first to share an office. It makes a big statement when the President and CIO, both owners, would give up their individual offices. More than that, we would allow our office to be used for meetings and not just our own use. It makes a further statement when you declare that your shared space is also a meeting room and leave it so others can use it.

The contrast with the previous owner's large private corner office with its own bathroom and separate reception couldn't be greater. It was also intentional. This sent a clear message that let people know that there was a new way of doing things. When the previous owner left, we inherited that extra space but instead of accommodating ourselves, we turned his office into a conference room and kept our modest shared office.

In the world of culture change, actions speak louder than words. We wanted the message to be clear. The new culture was more than words and it was here to stay.

Our leadership style has tried to demonstrate a new approach. We purposely have kept the idea that two leaders would share not just an office, but also decisions. We were forced to show how decisions should be made—by joint consensus and based on consideration of the facts and often in public and in real time.

Nothing we did was simple, and change didn't happen overnight. There were countless lessons to learn. Gradually, over time, people have learned, more and more, they had to argue facts and not opinions. They have learned that we are more concerned with outcomes and not as interested in politics. They learned that they could give their opinion, and all have the right to challenge any dictum, but that challenge must be fact based. They learned that data itself, without proper scrutiny, could still be challenged. Little by little we have broken down the previous culture.

Cultural change takes time. We didn't have enough time. We couldn't change it totally. But we focused on base hits not home runs, the way we have done everything else. The bottom line is if we are making progress, we can move forward while continuing to work on change.

We are imperfect and the culture will be as well. We also know there will be setbacks. We acknowledge these and try to find strategies to set us back on course. When the old culture of opinion, politics and defeatism rears its head we often turn to our focus to business intelligence, to gather data and use that to turn the discussion towards a fact-based investigation. To avoid finger pointing, we implemented a task management software that monitors the status of any task, and to find where there was inefficient 'back and forth' in our processes. Facts rule.

If someone says something is impossible, we'll structure an experiment and run tests to prove whether this is true. If the test proves the idea can't work, we don't try to deny the result. We point out that if you fail to try because you might fail, you'll miss great opportunities. When you do fail, however, it is not an excuse for not trying again with a different approach. Failing isn't a crime in our new culture. The crime is not learning from failures.

When experiments do not work, we use that as an opportunity to learn. We examine and try to figure out why it didn't work. Where possible, we try to make improvements or changes and see if that makes a difference. No blame. No huge expense. Our only instructions are to 'set goals, measure carefully and *'fail fast.'*

We won't win every battle or solve every issue. But by relentlessly pursuing the facts and learning from them we will eventually find ways to succeed together. We are making real progress. But life isn't always fair. Even as we made progress, and make progress, new challenges emerge.

Money is tightening up again. We've had some new sales successes, but nothing moves as fast you wish. Even today, we continue to search for ways to further accelerate our cultural change.

We have learned the real lesson of digital transformation. It never ends.

What We Did

We began the journey that we would later come to see as a digital transformation in 2011 when we stopped printing the magazines and broadsheet style publications that had been our stock and trade. Revenue was plummeting. Costs were rising for production, printing and distribution.

We didn't do this in the context of a full strategic plan. We attempted that on several occasions, but the landscape was changing so rapidly, the end state we were moving towards was so uncertain, and the organization was so problematic that strategic planning in the classic sense was impossible.

As we have noted earlier, we didn't think that we were doing anything as grandiose as digital transformation. We were simply trying to survive and get the organization on its feet. It was only with time that we could look back on our progress, our trial and error, our successes and setbacks; only then did we recognize the path that we had been following.

We thought it would be useful to summarize those actions and some of the lessons we learned that might be applicable and perhaps helpful to others on their journey.

Stop the presses, stop the bleeding
The first action that marked the beginning of the transformation of the company was the decision to end print. It was a bold but necessary move. We needed to take some immediate and drastic actions to restrain our costs. It was a simple but wicked problem.

A very large part of our revenue came from print, but no matter what we did we came back to the same issue. We were losing money on every unit we produced.

Stopping print would remove the expensive production and printing costs. It would also collapse our revenue and cash flow.

We replaced the print editions with digital editions of our publications. In the process learned a big lesson.

In the first few months the digital editions of our magazines did well in terms of both readership and even advertising. But after only a couple of editions readership fell and with that, sponsors lost interest. We learned that simply *digitizing the product does not create a digital transformation.* We found:
- our digital products reduced expenses but didn't replace all the missing revenue. Digital products lend themselves to hypercompetitive markets and commodification is always a threat. They will not replace an old revenue source dollar for dollar.
- digitizing a product only removes the direct costs of production and distribution of that product. Legacy companies have inelastic costs that are embedded in the organization. These do not disappear with digitization and only a total transformation of the organization and the business model it operates under will remove them.
- our brands and market presence were embodied in those physical products. The printed magazines were powerful symbols to our audiences. The digital publications and even the websites did not, in our assessment, manifest those brands and communities in the same way. In a digital world, we had to find new ways to develop and maintain our role at the centre of those communities.

Here are some of the strategies we tried. For our flagship CIO brands we:
- partnered with another large organization (ITAC), and focused on our Canadian CIO of the year award;
- created a new CIO Census to study the Canadian CIO;
- created a new CIO retreat following a different path;
- while event providers chose big venues and focused on audience quantity and presentations, we focused on smaller more intimate gatherings with a focus on real discussions and sharing among peers;
- worked to enhance our webinars and roundtables. Where we had formerly used a journalist to lead the discussions we shifted to facilitation by our CIO or guest CIOs from the community;
- given the choice to support our U.S. partner's CIO Council, we opted instead to take a risk and back the fledgling Canadian CIO Association.

Actively pursue new revenue sources

We tried many strategies to make up for the revenue we lost as print disappeared. We focused on other areas such as events, webinars and lead generation. These were important and might play a role in our future revenue, but we knew that our audience was core to our value, and we had to find new ways to deepen, analyze and eventually monetize our knowledge and relationships.

We worked in two areas. We focused on analytics and content as core areas of value. We developed new 'peer to peer' research and community activities with and for our key audiences.

These strategies aimed to keep us at the forefront of the audiences we wanted to serve. We had knowledge that no one else had, not of markets or products but of the IT decisions makers and influencers. Moreover, when we redefined our research and reporting as 'peer to peer' we distinguished ourselves from analyst firms such as IDC and Gartner. We also tapped into something very powerful and related to the new digital marketplace. In the digital and social era, peer reviews were one of the greatest impacts on purchasing attitudes. If we could make this work, we would define ourselves not as a commodity but as a differentiated and highly valued offering to our readers and our sponsors.

What we learned from the CIO offering we spread to other areas and communities in the world of IT and extending into related areas as well.

IT services and products are developed by a large number of companies. In effect, these corporations 'manufacture' the hardware, software and increasingly the 'as a service' products and services for use by companies of all sizes and industries. Many of these organizations sell directly. But increasingly, in IT and other industries, an enormous amount of the sales and service happens in what is called 'the channel.'

The channel is a massive network of vendors and providers who resell products and services across the country. While the industry is enormous—in Canada alone sales are in the billions—it had no organized presence or community other than our events and publications. Our strategy was to unite that group into a stronger presence, as we had done with the position of CIO when it was created in the 1970's. IT World Canada would champion the industry and the new role that was emerging, the 'Channel Chief.' We:
- created a not-for-profit association for the industry - the Canadian Channel Chiefs Council (C4);

- brought in all the major players and showed our commitment to this key audience and industry;
- revamped our two semi-annual events in partnership with C4;
- added events to focus on groups within the channel including a "Women in the IT Channel" event with recognition for the many women who are so important to the industry.

Once again, communities and peer to peer stories would feature highly in everything we would do. This strategy took time but has been successful and is even beginning to be recognized internationally. We continue to look for ways to apply similar strategies across new audience areas.

Cut the technology budget and build a new infrastructure

Our 'Catch 22' was that technology costs were a huge part of our expense problems, but we needed technology more than ever to build and support new digital services. If we failed to automate, our staff costs would skyrocket from manual processes and workarounds. As well, we had to offer an extraordinary reader experience to compete in a global market which required a major CMS refresh or even replacement.

Our web-presence also needed a serious upgrade to cope with the new offerings, new types of content and of course the new ways of accessing that content—mobile, tablets and others.

The budget crisis was an issue but, in some ways, it helped us. It made us more open to new ideas, more willing to take chances and more focused on execution. We:
- looked at alternative areas, tapping into the new open source or at least open standards-based offerings;

- adopted new low-cost commercial SaaS products, the largest move being our early move to Gmail and the free suite of collaboration products that come with it. Using these we have increased productivity and enabled remote work. In turn, we could reduce our physical office space and combat the traffic chaos of our city;
- consolidated our hosting by embracing virtualization and creating our own private cloud. This was not painless. We had issues and obstacles on all our systems. Particularly difficult, was having one big packaged application that was not setup to be virtualized. We persevered and found a way to make it work in our virtualized environment.
- redesigned our outsourcing arrangements to cut expenses and bring us to a much more stable technology infrastructure;
- renegotiated our outsourcing and hosting, consolidating to a single provider that had excellent service and who would help us virtualize and reduce our footprint. As we examine our costs today, this work has paid off. Our lower outsourcing costs and much higher reliability are directly related to our rationalizing and restructuring of our systems as we virtualized;
- used public cloud when it makes economic sense and not purely because it's the 'way to go.' We regularly benchmark each area. As late as last year we were still much more cost efficient with our private cloud. But we found a few key areas where public cloud was superior and at least cost competitive. This keeps us focused on continual improvement and our experimentation itself has value.
- brought in VOIP phones and other collaboration tools;

- moved our proprietary .NET CMS to an open source WordPress installation, using responsive design to enable us to serve all mobile devices as well as laptops and desktops. Our aim has been to create a seamless experience regardless of device or location. We've also built a lot of expertise and benefited from our early moves in this area.

Our cost reductions were impressive, and our infrastructure became an asset instead of a liability. We also built a small but much stronger team, one that learned how to succeed. We eventually replaced the Audience Services system with our own custom database using open standards and an open source framework and did it in an unheard of three month timeframe.

If we had to pick one decision that we made in technology; it was to put our faith in our team. We gave them the autonomy they needed, provided support when things went wrong and at the same time tried to provide the coaching and guidance to ensure they didn't get in over their heads. It was at times a challenge, but they always came through.

Finding Agility

We were not just a classic example of how good people deliver bad results in IT. Our entire organization suffered a similar fate.

In IT, we focused on features rather than the problems that people are trying to solve or the outcomes they are trying to accomplish. We presumed that automating everything was the solution to all our problems. At the conceptual level, it seems fantastic. But it never worked.

To truly become agile, we had to stop thinking about the 'business' and IT'. We had to stop looking for silver bullets and start focusing on outcomes that create value for the customer. Not all processes should be automated. Some should be totally reconceived, and some should simply be abolished.

We also found that the same approaches we used to get our IT house in order were applicable to the business.

We decided we would:
- find and eliminate the root cause of problems and learn that as an organizational discipline;
- focus on using a combination of Agile and Lean in the organization as we had in IT;
- tolerate no grand visions and big projects. Everything would start with a minimum viable product (MVP) and let the customer value guide us;
- start with measurable and provable outcomes that are of value to the customer and work back from there;
- benchmark the current state before starting any change and agree on not only what success is, but how it would be measured. Everyone must agree on an objective measurement of progress.

Our combination of Agile and Lean was critical to our success. We would never consider technology separate from the processes it enabled and the outcomes it served. We weren't automating a process. We were finding the optimal combination of technology and process that got the result we wanted. Everything had to be justified using major tenet of Lean:

Anything that a customer would not willingly pay for (given the choice) is waste.

We created a world where everything can be questioned. When someone would say, "we need to automate this step," we'd ask, "why do we even need to *do* this step?" When they'd say, "we need to have edits in the system that would catch this error," we'd ask, "why are we making this error in the first place?" When someone would say "we need a check or approval," we'd ask, "why we didn't just get it right in the first place?"

Process and Organization

As much as we wanted to, we finally had to admit that we could not support a full Lean process transformation. We simply did not have the resources to do it. So, we did the next best thing. We:
- focused on key areas where work was "handed off". In a siloed organization where fingers are always pointing, this is the one place to focus on;
- ensured every time work was passed from one area or person to another, we insisted that the person or area receiving it was entitled to everything they needed including clear instructions on what success looks like based on defined outcomes.

One of the key handoffs that never worked was between sales and operations. At least one of our salespeople was constantly in the operations area interrupting and trying to manage each step of the process. Instructions were not clear. No matter what we tried, we ended up in the same situation—things falling through the cracks, constant crisis and rework and the only reason we met deadlines at all was due to heroic efforts from some of our staff. This was not just inefficient; it was perpetuating everything we were trying to break down from the old 'siloed' and hierarchical organization of the past.

When we saw it in those terms, we had an idea that on the surface sounded crazy but might just work. At a time when we desperately needed sales, we took one of our key salespeople, Desere Ross, and put her in charge of operations. Des was knowledgeable, determined and very organized. She also had the credibility to address both sales and delivery. Her job was to ensure that the instructions passed on to operations were clear. If any corrections were needed, she would manage them.

This allowed us to get tighter control of all aspects of our hand-offs from sales to operations. Contracts and statements of work were clarified and put in the CRM to store these instructions and ensure everyone had access.

Things didn't change overnight. But our new head of operations was determined, and we supported her relentless drive and passion for improvement. We even went so far as to hire an outside coach for her to help her adapt to her new role and the career change it represented.

With this approach, we could see real and measurable progress. It promoted, or perhaps forced a collaboration between everyone involved in sales and delivery. More importantly, it started to build a 'win-win' attitude. No one could succeed by themselves. With clear instructions and her experience, where the process broke down was eminently clear to our new operations head.

Confronting our culture

We took a lot of steps to change our culture. Breaking down the silos was one of our chief objectives. We broke the IT and business silos with our Agile and Lean approaches. Moving a salesperson into operations helped to break down the sales and operations silo. We did a lot of other things over the months and years. We:
- changed the work environment. We took the opportunity to reduce our footprint and rent by moving into a smaller space. In the process, we cut costs, and were able to redesign in a way that supported a flatter organization. The

most visible symbol is that we parted with many offices and other symbols of hierarchical power. Offices were no longer symbols of power. Almost everyone shared an office, including the two major shareholders, the president and the CIO. It is not uncommon to see one or the other working at a cubicle or in a conference room so the other can take a meeting or conference call.
- focused on facts. No rumours. No blame games. Just facts. Each time someone would come in with a crisis, we insisted on the facts first and the discussion second.
- let people know the old toxic behaviour was not going to be tolerated. One by one we parted company with people whose behaviour was toxic, even when it caused us short term pain. We parted with a salesperson who was exceeding his quota, again at a time when we needed revenue. But his behaviour was toxic. He demeaned the operations staff, had constant anger issues and the toll that he took on the organization was simply not worth it.

In taking action, especially when it hurt, people understood that previous behaviors of the old authoritarian culture would simply not be tolerated. Getting rid of a couple of high performing, destructive personalities cost us in the short run, but in the long term it had a powerful positive impact on the culture. Equally, however, we have offered an olive branch to those who wanted to change, spending time and occasionally, precious dollars on coaching.

As we built up a new culture, more of the 'old guard' had decided that this was not the place for them. Sometimes it hurt to lose them. Surprisingly, however, others who had 'lived in the shadows' stepped up and impressed us with what they could do. We also lost some good people along the way, but each time we did we gave internal candidates the first shot at the job. We found that we were often surprised by how they stepped up into new roles.

Sometimes, we were forced to look outside. When we did, it took us a long time to find the right fit with new people. We made a couple of very strategic hires including a head of marketing and content creation as well as a new head of sales. We took the time to find just the right people and we had to make tough choices to fund these new positions, but having the right people was the right choice.

Slowly, painfully we have made real inroads. Today, we have retained part of our history and the best part of our old culture—the passion to do great work and to serve our audience and our customers. A number of key people have stayed with us. We have built a newer, more diverse, energetic and frankly a more fun place to work. Our new office is pleasant. The old toxic culture is, for the most part, a thing of the past. We will not return if, and only if, we lead in a new way.

Even though we worried about the loss of expertise, we have found talent that we didn't know we had and added others who have made astonishing contributions. Our clients respect us more than ever and regard us as experts that produce the highest quality work.

We learned the lesson that a strong team with a 'win-win' attitude will always perform better than a set of highly talented but ultimately dysfunctional individuals.

Strategy vs. Tactics
Every day we both come to work with a list of things that must get done urgently. Then we respond to the crisis of the day. There is always something. Financial pressures. Staff issues. Clients.

Getting to the bottom of that 'to do' list can seem impossible. So how do you get time to think beyond the tactical? How do you find a way to do real strategic thinking? We knew that we had to create a space to think beyond the day to day and get some perspective and longer-term thinking. Here's what we've tried:
- the two partners, Fawn and Jim, have a standing dinner appointment, once a week, away from the office. Sometimes those dinners have an agenda, sometimes we talk about items that arise. Each week, we have the freedom to imagine, converse and even debate how we can advance our strategy;
- we try, not always succeeding, to spend a half a day a week on strategic issues;
- we have similar meetings with key staff to allow us to have regular conversations solely focused on strategy and coaching and not just the day to day operational issues.

We speak frankly. We discuss. We dream. We even argue. But we get time to discuss items without interruption, to blue sky, to have a conversation, sometimes about difficult things. With this regular time planned away from the office, we know that if something needs a longer discussion, we have time reserved for it.

Leading and learning by example:
There's a great deal written in terms of leadership filled with platitudes like "walk the talk" and those sorts of pithy but useless phrases. We knew that we needed a new style of leadership that could take us through what was going to be stormy and difficult times. We needed to break the old models of hierarchy and work towards a team leadership approach. Neither of us are 'in charge.' We make decisions by consensus. If we wanted to flatten the

organization and have a distributed leadership model, we had to lead by example.

When people talk about "tone from the top" it's as if what we say is the most important thing. It's not what you say, it's what you do that counts. Things like sharing an office or telling staff that "their client work comes first and then, could they come to see you?"— those actions are observed, and lessons taken. Likewise, if you want a culture where you learn from mistakes, you need to admit when you've made them. We try.

It's easy to say and hard to do, especially when you are an owner of a business and your own money is on the line. We aren't perfect and we regularly talk about issues of our own leadership at our weekly meetings. We knew were on the right track, however, during a very stressful time when one of our staff pulled us aside and respectfully but firmly quoted our own words back to us. It was respectful and it was honest. When your staff are not afraid to speak 'truth to power' it's a sign that your leadership model is working.

Land what you launch

We've spoken earlier about the need to be honest about projects that are failing. The old idea of 'declaring a victory' or ignoring a failure—all too common in many companies—is like a vaccination against change. Some projects will fail or be stopped, and when this happens it requires transparency.

Equally, we must be tenacious. Hiding failures is wrong but giving up is equally problematic. The trick is to be honest when things are not going well. If the project must not fail, you have to change the approach. We came back to our CRM three different times with three different approaches. In each, we had to acknowledge what we had gotten wrong the last time and articulate why this would be different.

But we need to have the wisdom to know we can only do so much. We embarked on a Balanced Scorecard project with great planning and enthusiasm and found that we, like so many other companies, were great at launching these things, but not so great at sustaining them. That didn't preclude us from looking at why we'd failed and coming back with a different approach to achieve the same thing - keep us focused on measurable accomplishments. That's more difficult when what you are doing is something that is as famous as the Balanced Scorecard, but the reality is not that *it* doesn't work. It just doesn't work for us, currently. We needed metrics, but we had to be less grand in our plans. Perfection can be the enemy of accomplishment.

In fact, it's hard to think of any initiative we've started where we haven't had to do a reset and come back with a different, often smaller and more practical approach. But in the process, we have taken the company from a 'we tried that before and we failed' attitude, to 'we tried that and found it wouldn't work and why— so let's try again.' With the courage to honestly look at what hasn't worked and try again, we now have done a lot of things that we never thought we could do.

The final level of pragmatic maturity is something that we are still working on. When there is too much to do and too few resources to do it all, the mature response is to know where you choose to fail if necessary.

The first level of wisdom is to choose not to take on everything. The digital world is awash with potential and avoiding 'bright shiny syndrome' is essential. It's not easy and as one executive told us, "It's no longer a case of separating the wheat from the chaff. It's separating the wheat from the better wheat." We must only do what advances our strategy the most, and balance that with our capacity to do it. If you have to juggle five balls instead of three, you may drop one, no matter how hard you work. Try to pick the one that has the least impact. But whatever you do, once you drop one, let it go and focus on the four that are still in the air. Forgive yourself and move on. There's no other formula, and we, like everyone else, are a continual 'work in progress.'

Our new branding – 'The Content Experts'

We added the tagline 'The Content Experts' to change the emphasis from publisher to media house, from transactional commodity to creative producer of peer to peer content. With the importance of content in marketing we were determined to be the leading creators of digital content in the technology industry in Canada. We understand how to engage our audience.

We put Jim Love, our CIO, in charge of content expanding his mandate from CIO to Chief Content Officer. We hired a former head of Radio Drama at CBC, James Roy, to head our video and podcast creation. We recruited Steve Proctor, author and journalist, to head marketing and commercial content creation. Lastly, we attracted a skilled sales leader, Ray Christophersen, formerly of ComScore and the National Post, to round off the new team.

Fawn Annan remains president, CMO and is now also CEO of the company. Fawn is our ambassador, who builds national community partnerships with industry, agencies, associations and governments. When there was no association to partner with in this key area, she created the Canadian Channel Chiefs Council (C4) and has taken that organization through its growth and to the point where we are being studied by others around the world.

Today, we are no longer just journalists who do events and other lead generation activities. We have made our pivot. We produce and amplify all forms of content—white papers, resource kits, studies, surveys and case studies. We do this in text, video and audio forms. While our written content is extraordinary, our award-winning video continues to reach new heights in creativity and our client list grows. Two of our hit podcasts generate more than half a million downloads a year.

Our history is our strength, but it's also a weight at times. As we become more and more of a creative content producer we may be perceived as encroaching into the territory once held by creative agencies. To keep this separate, we invested in our own arm's length company, called the 'Amazing Agency!' Amazing! is a real agency that is earning its own reputation for highly creative content production. It's first project was a thirteen-episode television series. It continues to innovate and explore at the edges and is the video agency of record for one of the largest technology companies in the world.

We continue to experiment, learn and develop, having made the shift from a rigid hierarchical publishing company, to a dynamic, agile new media company. We will always have a focused passion for technology and what it can do. We still fail on experiments, but we get back up, dust ourselves off, learn and move on until we ultimately succeed.

And as we have truly come to realize, we can never stop learning. To be a digital company means to constantly look to adapt to the ever-changing expectations and needs of our customers and audience. Digital transformation is not an end. It's a continual process.

What We Learned

There is the old saying that "you only really learn from your mistakes." Yet all too many times business books lack in a frank discussion of what's been learned. Perhaps it's a reluctance to admit mistakes. Neither of us subscribe to that notion.

We're certainly not perfect. In fact, if you can take what we've done and find places where we've made errors or missteps and avoid those, we've succeeded in what we set out do with this book.

One question we've had to honestly address is this. Given that so many publishers have failed, what if we publish this book and our business fails at some future point? While the two of us steadfastly refuse to fail, we do admit the possibility exists.

Regardless of what the future brings, we firmly believe that nothing can negate the importance of what we have done and what we have learned. No matter what the future brings, we are confident that we are sharing things that are valuable and that we wish others would have shared with us when we began. We, unfortunately, had to learn almost everything for ourselves.

One thing we did learn—mistakes and all—was the real meaning and impact of digital transformation. As we have repeated many times in this book, when we started our journey together almost eight years ago, we didn't think we were doing something as grand as a digital transformation. We thought we were trying to save a failing business. It was only as we look back on what we did that we realized that we were digital transformation pioneers.

We hope we have given you a frank account of our journey. We've tried to do this being as truthful and objective as we can. To the degree we've been critical, we think it is important to note that we are commenting only on behavior. Humans are wonderful resilient creatures who respond differently in different contexts and have a capacity for change that we should never underestimate.

We can take a few criticisms and will live with them. But we hope we have not elevated ourselves at the expense of others. If that is the case, we would offer our sincere apologies and where the case could be made, we will address it on the website that accompanies this book. We're not trying to be heroes at anyone else's expense. We are trying to share a real experience.

We have freely shared what we have learned at each step of the journey - this book is part of that. We've also had the position as publishers to hear many other stories. Some of these are reported in our web publications. Some are featured in our roundtables and meetings. The very best make it to our 'Digital Transformation Awards'—our annual celebration of companies that have made great progress in their journey.

In this section, however, we'd like to leave you with some of our more unstructured and personal observations about digital transformation. These are the things we've learned, what we wished we'd done differently or tips that we think you might find helpful. At least it's what we've learned as of the date of publication. On the website we've created additional resources and will add new learnings as we encounter them.

Early movers have more time

Although we were the first B2B publisher to stop print and go totally digital, we wonder if we moved fast enough—not just in stopping print, but in starting on the digital transformation, and changing the business model itself. We'll never know for sure. But we do know this. If you wait until you are disrupted by a digital competitor, you severely reduce your ability to make the necessary changes. Transformational change takes time. Culture is inevitably involved, and cultural change cannot be rushed.

We would have preferred a little more breathing room instead of a plunging dive into the deep end of the pool. We had no choice. We were bleeding financially, on the verge of going under, and our owner was talking about bankrupting the company. Still, if we had moved earlier, while we still had stronger revenue, we might have kept or modified some print rather than cutting it all. The penalty for delay is extreme action with all its risks. We've paid that penalty. If you have a choice to start earlier, you may have other options.

Over the seven-year timeframe we've been working through the issues of our own digital transformation, and watching others work through their own. We've worked on a strategy that we wished we had the luxury to employ. It's based on a concept that we call the 'flip' and it's our idea of how to make your digital transformation be a smoother transition than ours, if you move early. It's the alternative to our 'guillotine version' of change where you get so far down the path that you only have one option—an abrupt stop to the legacy and a rapid shift into the new digital organization. Having lived on the blade edge of the guillotine we don't wish this on anyone.

If you can start early, you can start small. On a tiny scale, be your own disruptor before you make the full move or that move is forced on you. Use that experiment to learn and work out the issues. Yes, you will cannibalize some of your existing (and often profitable) offerings, but you can do this in a managed basis. Create MVPs and leverage small sections of your customer base, first on a pilot basis.

You can experiment with Minimum Viable Products (MVPs) and only move when you know you have it right. If you must fail, fail fast and learn. Then, in one way or another come back. If you are not planning your own disruption, someone else is.

You can gradually shift emphasis to the new product or service line while retaining your core customers, and even working with them to develop the new offerings. When you reach a critical mass, you are ready to 'flip' and do a phase out of the old line of products.

There will be a bit of abruptness to this 'flip,' but it is far superior to the roller coaster ride we were forced to take. For example, if we had started a digital version of our magazine and run it for half a year before making the shift, we may have learned some lessons much earlier and even found some ways to make the digital publications more sustainable. We don't know.

This would have saved us from a hard lesson when the digital edition was new and novel it got a lot of interest from readers, but it also died out after just a few issues.

It may have also helped us with another lesson where advertisers couldn't figure the value of a digital version. It was problematic in terms of sales. It wasn't a print ad and it wasn't a digital ad. If it had been an early experiment, it would have been easier to manage.

We might have learned earlier that you can't do everything digitally that you can do in print. We didn't learn, for instance, how much our key audience would miss the picture on the cover of our CIO magazine until we held our 25th anniversary and we heard that comment throughout the evening in the presence of over a hundred CIOs.

In the section *'What We Did'* we discussed some of the ways that we used to address this once we saw the impact of cancelling print. We could have done these sooner or even evolved different strategies had we known.

These are our specific lessons. Ours is a story about print. But there will no doubt be similar lessons for other products and services. We've seen some companies use similar approaches to move from existing products to an "as a Service" model. We've seen hardware providers confront similar issues, some waiting too long to respond. The struggle to change is not about the product or service. For hardware companies, the transition from a business model based on large purchases to one based on vastly lower but ongoing regular payments. The secret is to experiment early and learn before you are forced to move.

Digital Transformation is a change in the business model driven by an intense pursuit of a stellar customer experience and an authentic customer relationship. But no matter what product or service you provide; the shift is less painful and perhaps less risky if you have time to learn and evolve.

Digitizing is not Digital Transformation

It's easy to make the mistake of thinking that digitizing your products or services or even parts of your organization is a 'digital transformation.' It might be a step in that direction, but it's a false and misleading idea. Your competition is not beating you because they have a digital product. They are beating you for two reasons:

- their version of the product or service (digital or not) better meets an unspoken need or desire of the customer;
- they have created a new business model that gives them a permanent advantage in terms of not just cost, but in terms of their agility.

We learned this the hard way. We replaced print with a digital version of the magazines that were part of our brand. But we didn't 'transform' them or make changes to enhance the experience and truly exploit what the digital world could do. We reproduced them in a digital form. We didn't tackle our business model. We were late in transforming our organization—its processes and its culture.

We made the same mistakes that almost everyone does when they attempt to reproduce what they are currently doing in a digital format. At least initially, we treated the new world like it was simply a new digital version of the old world. In so doing, we were both frustrated by its limitations and blinded to new possibilities. The real secret is to see the new with new eyes. Only then do your truly discover the power of a new and transformed organization.

A real digital transformation of a product, service or company reimagines everything, not on fitting the old to the new format. It is focused on aligning everything from concept to production towards providing a fresh and engaging experience for customers. Understanding this is what makes the difference between a competitor with a digital product and a true digital disruptor.

Taxis had apps for phones before there was Uber. And to see Uber merely as an app that allows you to order a vehicle is to miss everything that made Uber disruptive. Uber tapped into a dissatisfaction with the taxi experience and set about to change every aspect of that.

Likewise, banks have had online banking for years, but the new Fintech companies that are emerging are more than simply an online version of the same frustrating banking experience.

One of the things that we did right, at least in our opinion, was to skip the common wisdom and the development of a mobile app altogether in favour of a total rethink of how to meet a reader's need for an exceptional omni-channel experience on any device. If we ever do an app, it will be because that's a superior way to meet the needs of our audience, not because others are doing it. That logic should pervade every decision. The question is not "what is everyone else doing." It's "what is the best way to create an exceptional customer experience?"

Digital disruptors truly transform every possible aspect of the product or service with a relentless focus on the customer experience. They tap into unmet needs. This is so powerful that even when they can only provide a portion of what their legacy competitor does, they are still able to take market share.

While we lost the cost of printing, we didn't tackle some of the real competitive threats early enough— other content producers, changes in the reading habits of our audience and other factors. These are things that we only learned over time and with experimentation. Had we always taken the approach that we wouldn't just replicate the analogue experience in digital form we might have launched differently.

Digital disruptors, while they align all their production towards the customer experience, also question every aspect of production starting with the business model and moving to the very nature of the business itself. This creates an agile competitor with an innovative approach that makes it incredibly difficult for the existing legacy companies to respond without transforming themselves.

Uber didn't own cars, didn't have full time drivers and didn't respect the licensing models that drove the taxi industry. Airbnb didn't try to be a virtual hotel. New Fintech companies serve only a small range of needs and a narrow sector of customers and refuse to be defined in classic terms. As we write this, Apple is coming to market with a credit card that has a twenty second application to approval. Without a legacy, or with courage to step outside their legacy, digital competitors can focus on the essence of customer experience and on only the most profitable customers, meeting their needs and desires better than anyone else.

While we changed how we showed our content, initially we didn't really change how we created it or even what content we created. We still tried to serve a broad audience with the same business model. We didn't solve the underlying problem of showing a real 'ROI' on our replacement digital publications. So, after the novelty wore off, we were back to square one. While costs of printing and distribution dropped, the cost of producing the content itself didn't change. That's a challenge that we continue to work on but, at least initially, we made the initial mistake and the 'original sin' of digital transformation that so many others have and will continue to make:

We had digitized our products without becoming digital.

Moving at the Speed of Culture

Until you are in the middle of a digital transformation, you don't realize just how many elements of your culture work to slow or even frustrate that transformation.

If you are trained in classical organizational change the idea of tackling cultural change is daunting. In classic organizational change, cultural change is a last resort. It requires strong leadership and a sponsor who will make the long-term commitment to the change.

These plans are top down and focused on the employees (also referred to as "targets"). The job of the change management team (the "agents" of change) is to get acceptance and buy-in or at least compliance with the new structure and new behaviors.

Digital transformation is different. We are trying to move from a restrictive and rigid organizational model to a more agile and adaptive one. The leadership must also change. That new state has yet to be invented, and it cannot be simply designed and mandated. There is no real 'new model' to present and get buy-in or compliance. There are only steps to an uncertain future state that leaders co-create with their team.

In the new transformation, humans lead humans. That requires courage, humility and above all, a sense of purpose.

What we want to change is not just what people do. We want to change how they think. We aren't as much looking for compliance with a plan, as in building a shared understanding so that we can have high levels of autonomy without anarchy. Culture is our new regulator and purpose is our new motivation.

So how do you allow autonomy and flexibility to continuously innovate yet maintain a high availability, intensely secure infrastructure that conforms with a vast number of regulations across the world? It is possible. AWS does it, as does Google and others. They do it with a relentless focus on a culture of both innovation and discipline. Their culture creates that impossible balance between following disciplined delivery processes while simultaneously actively questioning the way things are done.

It's one of those things that 'works well in practice, but not always in theory.' Autonomy and creativity are easy to embrace, but hard to make work in a practical setting.

Our success in this area, especially in the early days was mixed. We had a real team environment when it came to events. Everyone pitched in, regardless of rank. We produced and continue to produce extraordinary events because of this collaboration. In the heat of battle, a flat organization worked.

But in the office, even after we parted company with some of the most rigid and difficult people from the legacy culture, we continued to have many silos. Editorial, sales, operations and even our analytics area had invisible barriers despite the appearance openness and friendliness in our small office. In day to day production, things fell between the cracks far too often. We were a team in public and a privately owned, hierarchical group in the safety of our office. Titles, areas of authority and even until our big move, offices and other status elements were far more important than they needed to be.

In an authoritarian world, resistance is subtle and passively aggressive, but it's still there and it remains very powerful. There were lots of smiles and friendly conversation, until you stepped into someone else's turf. With our insistence on extinguishing the worst excesses of the toxic past, our office was and is more pleasant than the old combative culture, yet, initially at least, we masked and didn't fully address the deeper issues.

Our entire culture had to be reinvented or our transformation would never work. Not an easy feat for any company, but extremely hard for a company that has been an owner operated, hierarchical and frankly, often cruel, selfish and bitchy.

We discovered this, or at least the key nuances of it, as we moved forward. We changed and continued to change the culture to be more agile, relentlessly focused on customer experience and above all, data driven. We had great analytics we weren't using on a consistent basis to drive all our decisions. That too, is cultural.

We broke the idea of hierarchy from the very top of the organization. We were two equal leaders who would strive for consensus. If we could flatten the organization at the top, we could flatten in at every level.

This was a challenge. The two of us have widely different approaches, attitudes, skills and experiences. For two strong minded people, used to 'running their own show' this was a real learning experience. It was not without issues and even conflict. But we were committed to making a new type of leadership work. We continue to remain committed to this leadership model.

This approach has had a real benefit. Everything we do is filtered through at least two points of view. We moderate each other's weak points and accentuate our strengths. We have both learned a lot from each other in this process. We do what we want the company to do—we collaborate, we embrace our diversity and we co-create our future. We are totally dependent on the success of the other for our own success. There can only be win-win, a colossal change from the past.

Because of our work, the company culture and the company itself continues to change and adapt, exactly what an agile organization must do.

But when all else fails, when you lose your way, when you seek that 'north star'—*focus on the customer experience.*

Transformation never stops
Recently we attended a Gartner conference where there was a lecture on Digital Transformation. The presenter, a distinguished

Gartner analyst pointing out what he felt was a problem with companies who are embarking on a digital transformation stated that companies need to ask the question "what are you transforming into?"

Like any presentation from an industry expert, especially a person of this stature and experience, one must listen and evaluate what he had to say. Without negating the value of his point of view, we had to reflect that our learnings point to a different question. The question for us is not what - it's why. "Why are you transforming?"

It might seem like semantics but it's essential to understanding our point of view. *What* are you transforming *into* implies that there is an actual end state, something that you can predict and work to become. We're not sure that this is the case.

There may be periods of relative stability. There may indeed must be periods where you can rest and celebrate accomplishments and even harvest economic benefits. But we found that any 'end state' was temporary, illusive or worse, an illusion. More importantly, if we were honest, we couldn't have really predicted what it could look like.

To assume a goal is to invite a final achievement, a stop to moving forward, to questioning, to reinventing. It is to invite complacency, to lose the hard-won agility and to risk being disrupted again. We must learn that the disruptor can be disrupted.

Blockbuster video was the disruptor of the movie industry only to find themselves disrupted by Netflix. Kodak made copious bold shifts in its history, making big bets on new processes and being ahead of trends like colour photography. Fast forward a few decades and the organization had become so rigid that it fought against their own invention— the digital camera. In the process they bankrupted the company.

We found that although you don't or can't know what you want to become there is one thing you can know—'why.' When we ask the question 'why' we don't look for the end state, we look for the purpose. In this world, purpose is a much better regulator and far more stable and enduring than any goal.

Various states, offerings, products, structures are all achievable. But what is achievable inevitably moves rapidly from future state to legacy. Purpose is unattainable. No matter how close we come, it is a continuing guide to moving forward, not a destination. No matter what you have achieved, purpose will always push you to make it better. Purpose will help you understand what you do and what not to do. Without a manual, without a roadmap, purpose is your true north which shows you the way and pulls you forward.

Humans need a sense of purpose and a sense of accomplishment. Although we do not want to move to an ultimate destination, it is important that you find milestones to celebrate our progress along the way. In a purpose-driven organization, these milestones are different. We pursue what Kaplan and Norton called 'leading indicators.' Where the goal-driven organization looks to win the game, the purpose driven organization looks to continually make the 'perfect play.'

Focusing on winning or losing is the old paradigm of business, and it still has relevance, at least when you meet your shareholders, financiers or banker. But it turns out that it is not particularly useful for learning. Imagine trying to coach a team that fixates only on the end-result. What would that conversation sound like? Let's imagine it:

Question: Why did the other team win?
Answer: They got 10 runs or goals or whatever and we only got 5. So, they won.

That's how the goal driven organization sees the world. It's accurate. It's real. But it's not useful in coaching. It says nothing that would lead a team to improve. It only reinforces the fact that they are, unless they beat someone else, losers.

The purpose driven organization, the agile organization, doesn't worry about winning or losing. It worries about doing the right things, over and over, and always getting better at them. In every situation, whether winning or losing, the purpose driven organization asks, "how can we do that better?"

When we look back at why we started on this journey, our purpose was and is, to use our storytelling abilities so that the lives of our audience and our community would become richer. We help them learn so that they can make better corporate, career and maybe even personal decisions. That's our purpose. It never stops. That's the power of pursuing the 'why' and not the 'what.'

Where we are today

Our journey has taken us from the brink of financial oblivion and over the eight years that we have worked together, to where we are today. We will never see our achievement as complete. Our industry is in flux. The position of any publisher is precarious, let alone a mid-sized, niche publisher in a small market like Canada.

Yet, we took the company back from the brink and lived to fight another day. We have an excellent team and a commitment to push forward to greater levels of success. We are proud of who we are and what our team has accomplished, but never really comfortable, nor can we afford to be.

We've learned a great deal as we went through this journey. We've learned more from our mistakes than our successes. That's inevitable. What's important is that we stuck to our guns, persevered, and kept our purpose clearly in mind.

Whether your company is facing the uphill battle of transforming to meet the new demands of the market or coming out the other side and looking for your next challenge, we hope our story will inspire and help you along the way.

We wish you success.

Resources

We have tried to give you our first-person account of the journey we undertook. As we continually note in the text, we didn't set out to do a digital transformation - we set out to save a company.

It wasn't until long after we had begun that we began to actively study, write about and speak on digital transformation. With Jim being a consultant and Fawn going through her executive MBA (at the same time!) we found that over time we had developed or adapted tools that we have used either in our own situation or in some of the workshops we have held with others.

We share these freely with you in our resources site for the book. We have not published them in the text for several reasons. First and foremost, these are an evolving set of tools and resources unlike our story, which is historical and fixed in time. We wanted the ability to continually update and add.

Second, we want the opportunity to co-create selective new tools from interaction with others who have had similar experiences, be they readers or our audience at speaking engagements.

For all these reasons, we have made the kit freely available at our site www.dxfirstperson.com

Enjoy

Jim Love and Fawn Annan